Hipster Mattic

MATT GRANFIELD

HipsterMattic

ALLEN&UNWIN

First published in 2011

Allen & Unwin
Sydney, Melbourne, Auckland, London
83 Alexander Street
Crows Nest NSW 2065
Australia
Phone: (61 2) 8425 0100
Fax: (61 2) 9906 2218
Email: info@allenandunwin.com
Web: www.allenandunwin.com

Cataloguing-in-Publication details are available
from the National Library of Australia
www.trove.nla.gov.au

ISBN 978 1 74237 785 8

Internal design by Brittany Britten
Set in 11/15 pt Sabon by Midland Typesetters, Australia
Printed and bound in Australia by Griffin Press
10 9 8 7 6 5 4 3 2 1

MIX
Paper from
responsible sources
FSC® C009448
www.fsc.org

The paper in this book is FSC certified. FSC promotes environmentally responsible, socially beneficial and economically viable management of the world's forests.

To Rebecca, for being amazing,
and to Mum and Dad, who have admitted that if they'd let me
get the haircut I wanted in grade nine,
none of this would have happened.

CONTENTS

*That is what we are supposed to do when we
are at our best—make it all up—but make it up so
truly that later it will happen that way.*

Ernest Hemingway

CHAPTER 1
HIPTRODUCTION

Luckily I didn't own a bath. If I'd had a bath I would have been crying in it, and there were so many tears and so much snot the thing would have started overflowing and I would have floated out and broken a rib on the floor.

The shower had no plug, so I couldn't float out or do any wallowing of consequence, but it was still very snotty. At least the constant running water made it moderately hygienic. I didn't break a rib, but I did manage to pull a rib *muscle* while attempting to assume the foetal position in between two particularly violent moans.

There's a beautiful reprise in any major sobbing session when you take a deep sniff, run your index finger under your nose, pause for a second, frown emphatically and assure yourself the worst is over. It's a brief and snotty moment of solitude that arrives in the darkness like a lantern of hope and then exits swiftly and without favour, leaving you alone to whimper wildly in the shadows once more. I'd just reached that moment when her words echoed around me again.

'We're just two different people,' she'd said. This was over the phone—it had been a relatively short but tumultuous long distance relationship.

'Actually, it's not that we're different people, it's more that I'm a person and you're a child. You're fine when it's just us, but then you go out and end up skinny-dipping in some random water feature at four o'clock in the morning. I never know where you are. More to the point, *you* don't seem to know *who* you are. You don't know where you're going. You have no sense of commitment. I'm sorry. It's over.'

And that was that.

I thought we were going to live happily ever after and end up doing the sorts of things proper adult relationship people do, like choosing dinner sets, shades of Dulux and preparatory schools for our as-yet-unconceived children. She thought I belonged in preparatory school.

I went back to sobbing in the shower for a while. This helped somewhat. I could sob with way more gusto than any five-year-old. This gave me some comfort.

She did have one point. I didn't have a clue who I was. Nor any idea how to go about finding out. Nor any drive or purpose for doing so. Maybe I needed to go spend a year in an ashram or something. That worked for the Beatles. I didn't really like Indian food though. Lamb korma was OK, but lentils just weren't my thing. I could never be a vegetarian. I also didn't really enjoy sitting still for too long. I liked swivel chairs because if you got bored you could push away from your desk and spin around for a while. Ashram yoga probably wasn't the way for me to find enlightenment. A tub of chocolate YoGo yes; yoga, no.

I weighed up the other rational options before me. Running away to join the circus was out. I had no co-ordination, I wasn't good with small cats, let alone big cats, and I couldn't put up a tent. Joining the French Foreign Legion was also a no-go for the same reason: camping wasn't my thing. I didn't much like shouting either. Moving to Cambodia to set up an orphanage was something I'd considered, but my friend Holly had looked into it and said all the good orphans had already been taken by Hollywood movie stars. There were other types of international volunteering of course—there'd been a few earthquakes and floods happening about the place—but they were mostly in organised countries and things seemed to be pretty much under control already. I wasn't sure what skills I could offer anyway. I'd managed to put together a set of IKEA shelves once, but that was the upper limit to my re-construction and engineering experience. I was fairly certain no one at the Fukushima Nuclear Power Plant was sitting around going, 'Fuck, if only we had someone with an arts degree to come up with a social media strategy for this.'

Everyone else I knew seemed to have their shit sorted by now. My other 30-year-old friends all had careers and partners and puppies and paint rollers. I had a couch and a bookshelf and a guitar collection. I'd had dinner with my high-school girlfriend and her husband a few nights previously and they'd been making plans to buy their second investment property. My idea of investing for the future was keeping a tin of tuna in the cupboard in case I got sick one day and couldn't make it to the shops.

My ex-girlfriend was right. I was a child.

The only friend who had as little to show for his thirty years of existence as me was my best friend, Dave. He lived in Sydney so I didn't get to see him as much as I would have liked, but he was always good for a phone chat whenever I needed him.

'Dude,' he'd said when we'd been hanging out the weekend before. This was after quite a few pilseners. 'You know I'll always be there for you. I don't care if it's three o'clock in the morning and you're on the other side of the world, if you need me, just call. OK?' He'd just been through a break-up himself, so I'd been consoling him and we were talking about how we'd always be there for each other. I didn't have a watch on in the shower, but my guess was about two-thirty in the morning. It was time to test the friendship.

I got out of the shower and dried myself off. All the bits that would dry, anyway. (My eyes and nose were in a semi-permanent state of damp.)

Dave's phone rang for a while and then went to message bank. I left him a message consisting mostly of sniffing and then called again. It went to message bank so I left another message apologising for calling so late and called again. He didn't answer so I left a message apologising for leaving so many messages. I waited thirty seconds and dialled again.

'What?' He finally picked up. He didn't sound very happy to hear from me.

'Hey mate, did you get my message?'

'What message?'

'Oh, I just left you a message.'

'What did it say?'

'Oh, I was just apologising for calling so late and leaving so many messages.' I said.

'Awesome. That was very considerate of you. I appreciate that. Thank you.'

He hung up.

I called back.

'What?'

'Hey, I just got dumped.'

'Oh dude, I'm so sorry to hear that. Can we talk about this in the morning?'

'It is the morning.' I had a point.

'I was thinking more *morning* morning.'

'Man, I'm really upset.' I made my voice crack a little so he'd be more sympathetic. 'I've been thinking about killing myself, hey.'

'Oh, what? No, don't do that. Really?' He sounded concerned now.

'Well, no,' I said. 'No, not really. I was considering opening my emergency tin of tuna though.'

He groaned. 'You're a dick. Did this just happen?'

'No,' I said. 'She called me this afternoon.'

'I see,' Dave said. 'Why did you wait until two-thirty am to call me then?'

'Is it exactly two-thirty?' I asked.

'Well, it's . . .' I could hear him shuffling around in bed to look at a clock. 'Two thirty-seven,' he said.

I'd always been good at picking the exact time. At least I had some skills. That's something I could do, I thought— go overseas to where people had suffered disasters and had no clocks and let people know what the time was. Obviously my judgement was a little off now, but there were extenuating circumstances. When I was back on my

A-game my abilities would be in high demand. I made a mental note to look at time-telling opportunities with the Red Cross when I got off the phone to Dave.

'Well, what happened?' he asked.

I told him.

I could hear him nodding on the other end of the line and making the appropriate 'oh', 'ah' and 'bitch' noises.

'She's right though. I have no idea who I am. I need to know how to find out. You were seeing that therapist guy for a while. What do I do?'

'It's not as simple as that,' he said. 'You can't just figure it out in a second. Buddhist monks and religious leaders and yogis spend their lifetimes trying to find out.'

'Yeah, well I'm not doing yoga,' I said.

'Heaps of hot chicks do yoga,' Dave reminded me.

I hadn't thought about that. Maybe I could do some yoga.

'Anyway, there's no magic trick or anything. You need some time to do some soul searching.'

I didn't like that answer. I needed results. Now.

'Can't you just give me something? Some little bit of advice to set me on my way? I've been crying for hours; I need something to take my mind off everything,' I said.

'There is one thing you could try,' he said.

'Yes! Good, what? Tell me tell me . . .'

'OK, so there's this little exercise my therapist got me to do when I first saw him. What you do is . . .' he yawned.

'Dude, tell me!'

'Sorry,' he said. 'OK, so write down what you did last weekend.'

'Is that it?'

'Yes, well, not just the main things, write down everything. Who you hung out with, what you bought, what you saw, where you went. Everything. It'll be a little window into the kind of person you are and then you can use that information to work out what you're doing and what you should be doing. Do that and then call me back tomorrow at a normal hour and we can chat.'

I thanked him.

This sounded easy enough. Easier than yoga, anyway.

I dried myself off completely and went to find a pen and some paper. A girl I once dated had given me a Moleskine notebook which I'd never really used and it had an official, journal-like, existential quality about it. It would do nicely.

I thought about what I'd done the weekend before. There was certainly nothing of consequence. I hadn't saved anyone's life or anything. It was all just little mundane weekend things. Still, Dave seemed to think it would help. So I wrote out the list.

On the weekend I:

- Rode a friend's fixed-gear bicycle
  ~ in Surry Hills.

- Went to a gig
  ~ of a band I hadn't heard of, they were pretty good, SO trying to be Radiohead though.

- Attended a photography exhibition
  ~ and Tweeted about it a bit.

- Bought a necklace with a large retro camera on it made from beads as a present for my friend who is a twenty-year-old photographer.

- Drank pear cider
  ~ on a grassy knoll
    ~ with a bunch of friends who worked at national indie radio station
      ~ while reading a classic hardback novel
        ~ and had to explain thick-rimmed underpowered Wayfarer spectacles did in fact have prescription in them.

- Played Scrabble on my phone with Dave, even though he was sitting opposite me
  ~ in a vegan café
    ~ in Surry Hills
      ~ and moaned about our jobs in advertising
        ~ while convincing girlfriend (bitch)
          ~ to work on her personal brand
            ~ then came home and blogged about it.

And that was it really.

I called Dave back.

'Dude, I said call me back at a reasonable hour,' he said.

'It is a reasonable hour,' I said. 'You're the one being unreasonable.'

He sighed. 'What did you come up with?'

'Well,' I said. 'I forgot to tell you, but after we hung out at that café last weekend I bumped into this homeless guy and he said he'd read my fortune if I gave him a dollar. So he looked at my palm and said I was destined to save people's lives and at that point I heard a woman scream from a third-floor balcony window and there were flames coming out behind her, so I scaled the outside of the building and carried her down to safety and she thanked me for saving her and I realised that I really want to be a fireman, and that I've always wanted to be a fireman, but that father would never let me be a fireman because he wanted me to go to university and get an arts degree because his parents could never afford to send him to university to get an arts degree, but I realised I never wanted to have an arts degree, so I'm going to go to fireman school and become a fireman.'

Dave sounded sceptical, but impressed. 'Hey man, that's really cool.'

'Yeah,' I said. 'I might have made a bit of that up. The fireman part. And the homeless man part. I did see someone in a window though.'

'Right,' said Dave. 'You do like to climb things so I wasn't quite sure.'

He was right. I did like to climb things. I tried to climb a fridge once. There was another skill for the international disaster relief effort. Fridge-climbing.

'So, what did you really do last weekend? Read me the list.'

I read him the list. He liked the bit about playing Scrabble on the phone while he was sitting opposite me. And the personal branding bit. And the thick-rimmed, underpowered spectacles bit.

'So,' I said. 'What do you think? Do you know who I am? Anything in there for you?'

He had a think about this for a while.

'Actually,' he said after some time. 'Yes. Yes I do.'

There was more silence while he considered his opinion. It sounded like he'd stumbled onto something and wanted to turn it over in his mind a while before he let me in on it.

'Well?' I said.

'Well,' Dave said. He was hushed. 'You're a bit of a fucking hipster, aren't you?'

There was silence for about twenty seconds while we both thought about this.

'I am not a fucking hipster!' I said, indignant.

'You're a massive fucking hipster,' Dave said. 'In fact, you're probably the biggest fucking hipster I know.'

'I'm not!'

'You're as hipster as it gets,' he said.

'No, I'm not,' I said.

'Yes, you are,' he said.

I said 'not' again. He said 'are' again. This went on for some time.

'I don't even own an Apple computer!' I protested. 'I don't drink coffee and I hadn't even been on a fixed-gear bicycle until last weekend when you lent me yours!'

Dave pointed out the fact that I wore thick-rimmed Ray Ban Wayfarer-style designer reading glasses, Converse sneakers, a bicycle courier-style bag, which usually had a copy of a classic American novel in it, that I worked in advertising as a day job, and that I spent an inordinate amount of time Tweeting about photography exhibitions.

'In other words,' he said, 'hipster. And there are thousands, perhaps millions of cool young things like you out there all over the world, sitting in cafés, drinking fair trade coffee, reading literature, writing what they hope will one day be literature, taking photos of people in floral dresses, starting ambient electro bands no one has heard of, wearing thick-framed glasses, going to music festivals and pretending to be, generally speaking, hip.'

'I'm not a hipster,' I said.

He thought about this.

'Actually, you know what? You're right. You're not a hipster. You're actually not cool enough to be a proper hipster.'

'Hey,' I said. 'I'm cool. My mum says I'm cool.'

'No, you're not,' Dave said. 'And even if you were cool, you're too half-hearted to be a hipster. You don't have the commitment. Your girlfriend was right. You're not a hipster, you're a halfster.'

He had a point.

'OK then,' I said. 'Maybe you're right. Maybe I should quit being a hipster altogether and go start some new sub-culture. Is that what you're saying? Do my own thing. Be myself. Yeah?'

Dave considered about this for a while.

'No,' he said. 'No, you can't quit being a hipster now. You've got to where you are because you like books and you're reasonably fashionable and you do all that stuff anyway. Quitting being a hipster isn't the answer. Quitting now would be like getting to Everest base camp and saying, "OK, that's high enough, I might turn around." If you

really want to find yourself you need to get to the top of
Everest. You need to stop doing things half-arsedly and
become the ultimate expression of who you are. You need
to become the *ultimate hipster*.'

I thought about this for a moment. It actually made
sense.

'I'm right, aren't I?' Dave asked.

I nodded.

'Are you nodding?' he asked.

'I'm nodding,' I said. 'So what does the ultimate hipster
look like? What do I do?'

'Well you could get a fixie for a start,' he said. 'You liked
riding mine: remember how fast it was?'

I liked that idea.

'What about an ironic tattoo?' he said.

I'd always wanted a tattoo.

'Hey,' I said. 'I could make pieces of jewellery out of old
board-game tokens and sell them at a market stall, along
with some organic vegetables.'

'Now you're talking,' Dave said.

'Get a free heirloom tomato with every Monopoly dog
ring.'

He liked that a lot.

'I could do heroin or something in the name of art.'

Dave thought it might be best if I didn't take heroin or
something in the name of art. I promised him I wouldn't.

We discussed the possibility of doing some street art
instead. I told him about an idea I had of writing inspira-
tional messages onto the walls of a train station using
nothing but soap. Technically it wasn't graffiti because it

was actually cleaning dirt off, so you couldn't get in trouble with the police. You could do the same sort of thing with sand on a beach if you wanted to—stay up until four in the morning and use food dye to write messages that everyone would see and then the ocean would just wash them away.

He asked me what sort of messages I would write and I said I wasn't sure yet but that they would probably involve some sort of stencil or something. Like Banksy.

'It sounds cool,' Dave said. 'But it's all a bit too much effort. Hipsters don't have that much motivation. Banksy isn't a hipster, he's an artist. There's a massive difference. Hipsters need to be artistic in some way, but they can't be too motivated.'

He was right.

'If you want to put effort into something, grow a beard,' he said. 'And then take your beard and hang out in trendy cafés and write poetry. That'll kill three birds with one stone.'

'But I've got a beard,' I said. I was quite proud of my neatly trimmed man-stubble. It was the most masculine thing about me.

'Mate, you haven't got a beard, you've got a five o'clock shadow. If you're going to be the ultimate hipster you need to look like you've just robbed the Glenrowan Hotel.'

'Is that what the ultimate hipster would do?' I asked.

'Yes. I think so. Yes,' Dave said. 'That's what the ultimate hipster would do. Now. Go and get some sleep. That's another hipster thing. Hipsters love sleep. Sleep is cool.'

I thanked him and hung up. I felt good. And I'd stopped crying.

CHAPTER 2
HIPSTERATURE

The term 'hipster' was coined by a New York musician in the 1940s. The Second World War was raging, jazz had only recently been invented and a new language called 'jive talk' was evolving in the underground piano bars of Harlem. If someone talked the lingo, they were referred to as being 'hep to the jive'. Around this time a young pianist decided he needed a stage name, so he changed the spelling of 'hep' to 'hip' and called himself Harry 'The Hipster' Gibson. The moniker caught on and *hipster* became proverbial for young, in-the-know scenesters who were at the pointy end of popular culture.

The term remained underground in New York throughout the 1940s, but as the 1950s rolled around, poets like Jack Kerouac and Allen Ginsberg adopted *hipster* as their own and wore it as a badge of resistance to the suburbanised Coca-Colony that mainstream America was becoming. It became a byword for those who saw themselves as artistic, individualistic and hedonistic. As the Beat Generation grew up, got day jobs and had babies, their flower children borrowed the prefix and became hip*pies*.

Inevitably, 'hip' ran its course and the term was shelved shortly after Woodstock. Any long-haired, marijuana-smoking acoustic guitar players who weren't scared into communes by Ziggy Stardust and Freddie Mercury were eventually shot by the Sex Pistols at the end of the 1970s. The following two decades were so full of cocaine and Kurt Cobain that no one had time to be hip at all, but by the turn of the twenty-first century a new counter-culture had started to emerge.

While mainstream society of the 2000s had been busying itself with reality television, dance music, and locating the whereabouts of Britney Spears's underpants, an uprising was quietly and conscientiously taking place behind the scenes. Long-forgotten styles of clothing, beer, cigarettes and music were becoming popular again. Retro was cool, the environment was precious and old was the new 'new'. Kids wanted to wear Sylvia Plath's cardigans and Buddy Holly's glasses—they revelled in the irony of making something so nerdy so cool. They wanted to live sustainably and eat organic gluten-free grains. Above all, they wanted to be recognised for being different—to diverge from the mainstream and carve a cultural niche all for themselves. For this new generation, style wasn't something you could buy in a department store: it became something you found in an opportunity shop or, ideally, made yourself. The way to be cool wasn't to look like a television star: it was to look as though you'd never seen television.

The prophets of this new religion were fashion bloggers, certain independent magazines and alternative radio stations. Their power and influence in hipster circles rendered French *Vogue* and MTV out-dated and irrelevant. If I was to become the ultimate hipster, they would be my bibles. Now, my ex-girlfriend worked for the biggest hipster radio station in the country. Given that facial hair is cool and follicley-inclined hipsters indeed do tend to emulate either bushrangers or adult-film icons from the 1970s, she was always bugging me to grow a crop of my own. I'd made a few conciliatory attempts, but it had always ended in me pulling out the clippers when either the itch on my upper lip became unbearable or a colleague had taken me aside and politely asked if I knew there was a strawberry Chupa Chup hanging from my chin.

Most men have sported a moustache at some point in their lives and secretly relish any excuse to let their upper lips answer the call of the wild. The love affair begins with the first dusting of post-pubescent fluff and rears its head again at various points in a lifetime—charity mos are popular, end-of-season football-trip growths are common and every now and then a costume party will present a man with the opportunity to dress as a member of the 1974 Ashes team.

Moustaching can be a good thing. It makes some men look rather dashing. When I give it a try, the result is caterpillars pashing. No man in my family looks terrific with a 'tache. On the other hand, my mother has never seen my father without a beard, and I'm evidence he has been able to get laid, so clearly at least some kinds of facial hair have been favourable to the Granfield clan. If I was to become the ultimate hipster poet I needed to pick either cheek or lip and get some hair on it. At least, given the caterpillar thing, the choice was obvious.

Beards and books have always been bedfellows. Socrates, Shakespeare, Tolstoy, Hemingway—rattle off a list of the world's greatest male authors and they're almost all guaranteed to have a chin rug. Maybe it's because they're too busy writing to shave. Maybe they're just lazy. I didn't know either way, but at least I knew my chin was in good company. Growing a beard wasn't a particularly gruelling task either. All I needed to do was avoid razors for a few weeks. As challenges went, it wasn't exactly up there with polar exploration. (Although if I let my face follicles sprout untopiaried I was sure to end up looking a little something like Sir Douglas Mawson.)

If crafting a beard was the easiest assignment on my path to ultimate hipsterdom, crafting poetry was potentially the hardest. I hated poetry. Once in high-school English class we'd had to analyse a book of prose by a famous Australian author and I'd flat-out refused on the grounds that it was irrelevant and uninteresting. When it was made clear to me refusal would end in suspension, and that suspension would mean I couldn't go on grade-twelve camp, I ended up writing a thesis on how our school should have been preparing us for the modern world by asking us to examine the subtext of Coke commercials instead of second-rate post-modern poetry. I failed the assignment, but they did let me go on grade-twelve camp, which resulted in Ineke Kay letting me touch her boobs, so it was a win in the end.

Dave was right though: I needed a serious artform to pursue. I couldn't crayon my way out of a kindergarten colouring contest and I was too scared to graffiti anything of significance. If I was committed to the cause I needed to get myself to a café and bust out some rhymes in an artistic yet lethargic manner. Ernest Hemingway did his best work at Le Rotonde in Paris, and while I didn't have any iconic watering holes in walking distance, there was a cosy little coffee shop around the corner which had second-hand books for sale, cute waitresses and an array of organic buckwheat pancakes. It was breakfast time on a Saturday morning, the in-crowd was milling and I had no excuses, so I grabbed my Moleskine and headed for the door.

I hadn't written a poem since primary school; I wasn't sure where to begin. I knew the less a poem rhymed, the more artistic it was, so that was a good starting point. I was pretty certain punctuation was optional too—or if you were going to include it, it had to be in inappropriate places, like between letters. Or better still, above léttérs. Alliteration was also good, from memory.

I tried to think of other formal-sounding literary devices we'd been taught in school so I could include them in my poem too. I hated formal-sounding literary devices as much as I hated poetry, so in grade eleven Andrew Stone had bet me $2 I wouldn't stage a protest by saying 'Onomato-fucking-poeia' in my oral presentation. I'd won the bet, so I'd have to throw one of those in for Andrew.

I was tossing up whether or not to buy myself some sort of fancy fountain pen, or whether it was more hipster to use (ironically) a mass-produced Biro when the waitress came over and took my order. I asked her to double check whether the buckwheat pancakes were organic. She assured me they were before she noticed my leatherbound notebook.

'Hey, what are you writing?' she asked.

'Oh, it's nothing really,' I said, looking academic and rubbing my newly-elongated stubble. 'Just a poem.'

'Oh cool!' the waitress said. She seemed impressed. 'What's it about?'

I hadn't thought about that at all. I gazed wistfully into the distance and then closed my eyes for a few seconds before exhaling. There was a breeze picking up outside and it was rustling some old newspapers around.

'Well, it's complex,' I said. 'But it's about the wind really, and how our dreams are really just at the mercy of the breeze.'

The waitress sighed. 'I feel like that sometimes,' she said. 'What's it called?'

I hadn't thought about this either.

I could see one of the newspapers had an ad in it for a gay and lesbian art show based on toilet graffiti. The poster was a little silhouette woman, like you see on the door to the women's toilet.

'"Paper Dolls",' I told her.

The waitress nodded. 'It sounds lovely. I wish I could write like you, you know. I'm just not very creative and all.'

'Here,' I said. I walked outside, picked up the newspaper, carefully tore out the woman's silhouette and handed it to her. 'For you.'

She smiled.

'Oh, why thank you,' she said. 'That's very sweet.'

'You're welcome,' I said.

'Did you want some coffee with your pancakes?' She asked. 'On the house.'

'No thank you, I don't drink coffee,' I said.

'All right then, won't be long.' She skipped off out the back somewhere, paper doll in hand.

I gazed back at the notebook. Poetry wasn't as hard as I'd thought. And judging by that little exchange I was also obviously going to be very good at it. All I had to do now was write something. I found a crisp new page in the notebook and began to compose . . .

Constructing cut-out versions of me:
Tattered newspaper. Torn in delivery.
  Torn to deliver me.
Different hopes, different dreams, different screams.
Snip
Sn.ip.
Thrown up. Up. Into the wind and away.
Holding my breath while I see where they land;
We dance like ballerinas.
The paperweightress and I.

I read it back to myself softly, but with a slightly louder rising inflection on the second 'up'. It seemed OK, in that it made me want to slit my wrists for boredom. It certainly didn't rhyme, so it was almost definitely art. I imagined myself reading it out aloud in a dark, smoky Paris café: a glass of cognac in my hand; bereted French girls swooning as the moonlight danced on their soft cheeks. Poetry was cooler than I remembered.

I decided the best thing to do would be to post it up on Facebook as a bit of show and tell. I had a lot of artsy friends and I was sure they'd appreciate my prose. It was only short so it wasn't like I was asking people to read a doctoral thesis or anything.

I wrote the poem as a status update and sipped some water while I waited for the praise to stream in. I'd recently added the editor of a literary review journal as a friend as well, so I wasn't going to be surprised if she dropped me a line asking if I'd like to publish my work in an upcoming edition.

Sure enough, it didn't take long for two responses to flow in simultaneously. Sam was my boxing class buddy. He was a really smart guy, so I was glad he'd taken a moment to chime in. Renee was my best friend Dave's flatmate. She was super-intelligent, but blonde, so I always made blonde jokes about her. I really valued her opinion though. Their comments were as follows.

Renee: Gay

Sam: Gay

Sam: Sorry Renee, you beat me to it.

Renee: That's OK. We can't underestimate how gay that was.

Sam: Correct Renee. Matt—I'm going to punch the gay out of you next time we're at boxing.

Me: It's deep, Renee. You wouldn't have the attention span to understand. I realise you're probably bored of this conversation already so here's a video of some puppies. http://www.youtube.com/watch?v=7bcV-TL9mho It's one minute and ten seconds. See if you can make it to the end.

Renee: Puppies are gay.

Me: You're gay.

Renee: You're gay. I'm bored with all this facebooking. I might go cut little paper people and throw them in the air and twirl like a ballerina!

I waited a while to see if anyone else chimed in. Someone 'liked' Renee's comment, but that was about it. The waitress did wink at me though. I wondered if it was too soon to add her on Facebook. I decided it was probably a little too soon, so I hung around to finish my breakfast and then left. At least my beard had probably grown a little bit while I'd been writing. That was something. It was starting to get a little bit itchy, and I was tempted to give it a trim, but I remembered what happened to Sampson when he had a haircut. I didn't want to lose all my hipster powers, so I persevered.

I went home and spent the rest of the day reading poetry online for inspiration while trying not to fall asleep. It all seemed a bit deep and boring. I looked up who the most hipster poet was and everyone seemed to agree it was Allen Ginsberg. He had a poem in the 1950s called *Howl* which talked about sodomy and drugs a lot. I wasn't much into sodomy or drugs, but I noticed that he liked to repeat things for emphasis, so I figured I could probably give that a try and see if it worked for me. Sylvia Plath and her knitwear also seemed pretty popular, although she ended up killing herself, which was sad. Still, at least she got Gwyneth Paltrow to play her in a movie, which was a pretty decent compliment. I thought about who I'd get to play me in the movie about my life as a hipster poet. Bill Murray was probably a bit old, so I settled on Jeff Goldblum.

The next day when I came back to the café the waitress had been replaced with a surly-looking tattooed gent. He didn't offer me any free coffee, so I ordered something with quinoa and settled in to write again, ignoring everyone.

I decided that if I was going to be a proper poet I should actually try expressing some real feelings rather than making them up based on newspaper ads. If I couldn't get a decent poem out of broken-heartedness then I wasn't going to get a decent poem out of anything. I felt Sylvia Plath would approve, although her creative technique also involved sticking her head in the oven, so I didn't know if I wanted to channel too much of her style. Still, I'd donned a cardigan I'd stolen from my grandpa's closet for a fancy dress party; she would have dug that.

I turned to a fresh page in my notebook and thought about how I felt.

I felt broken. So I started with that.

Today I am broken.
Shattered into uncountable pieces.
A god I cannot understand has taken me apart piece
  by piece so that I am nothing but dust drifting in a
  storm.
All I have are a few scraps of faith and instructions
  from a maker to re-build.
There is a thread of hope that tomorrow the sun will
  rise again, like it has done before.
I will look back on today and know that today was the
  day I started again with nothing but those scraps of
  faith and that thread of hope.

*I will know that today was the beginning of something
  new.
But today I am broken.*

I read it back. It seemed a bit sad, but I was a bit sad, so
I figured that was OK. I liked how it repeated stuff at the
beginning and end. That was very Allen Ginsberg. It had
more metaphors than the one from the day before, and it
still didn't rhyme: those were good signs too. I put it up on
Facebook and waited to see what other people thought.

Dave called me almost immediately.

'Hey mate, what are you doing?' he said.

'Hey, I'm at a café, writing poetry. Like you said. I haven't
shaved in a few days either. The beard's looking good,'
I replied.

'No, I mean, with all the sad poetry, what are you doing?'

'What do you mean?' I asked. 'I just went through a
break-up. I was expressing myself.'

'Dude,' he said. 'Everyone's just going to think you're
gay. Not that there's anything wrong with that.'

'Yeah, I noticed that,' I said. 'What should I be writing
then?'

'Well, lay off the Sylvia Plath for a start,' he said. 'Look
what happened to her. Ended badly. Oven.'

'Well, she was pretty depressed, I think,' I replied. 'I'm,
like, sad, but I'm not going to top myself. I haven't even
opened my emergency tuna yet.'

'Oh, that's good.'

'So what, liven it up a bit you think?'

'Yeah, give that a crack. And make it longer too.'

'Longer?'

'Yeah, *Howl* is like three thousand words. Aim for that.'

I said I'd try.

I pushed the pen around for a bit and tried to come up with something else, but one bit of prose was all I had in me for the day so I paid the bill and left. I tried to think about how Jeff Goldblum would walk if he was emulating my walk, and I walked home like that.

When I came back the next day I was still pretty down, but I was full of ideas. I had a vision of an epic hipster poem about going to see live bands and travelling the city streets on a bicycle and that sort of thing, but I just didn't know where to start. I had the cardigan on again but it was washing day so I had to grab an old band T-shirt from the emergency pile in the cupboard. It was a bit tatty, but I figured that made it cool enough. I ordered a green tea and browsed some of the second-hand books on the shelf for inspiration. I found a collection of Robert Frost's work so I grabbed that down to have a read.

It was a bit musty and made me want to sneeze, so I was about to put it back on the shelf when a little insect ran out of the spine and onto the table. I jumped back in alarm. I'd never seen anything like it before in my life.

'What the hell is that?' The cute waitress from the other day was back. She sounded surprised, and a little weirded out. Which I took as a good sign—you don't want to be eating in a café where the waitress's response to an insect running around the place is 'Oh god, not one of those again.'

We stared at it for a while.

'Actually, I think it's a silverfish,' I said.

'Oh, I've heard of those. I didn't realise they even existed,' replied the waitress.

It was real all right. It didn't much like the spotlight though, and it quickly scampered under the table and then out of sight.

The waitress shrugged.

'Weird,' she said. I agreed. She noticed my notebook again. 'Hey, what are you writing today? Another poem?'

I told her I was trying to write a cool poem, but I didn't know what it was about or how to start.

'Doesn't sound like a very good poem,' she said. 'No offence.'

I agreed with her. 'You got any ideas then?' I asked.

'What, for a cool poem?'

I said yeah.

She shrugged again. 'That silverfish was pretty cool. Write about that.'

I shrugged. It was worth a shot. I liked the idea that the insect was somebody's invention, so I picked up my biro and started writing.

Oh, little leviathan of the insect kingdom
I thought you were a myth, like Robin Hood in England
I thought you'd been made up as a bit of a joke
By a graphic designer named Alan, who smoked.
Pencil in hand and a pipe in his jaw,
He'd sit there all day with labels to draw.
Some were for fly spray, some for repellent.
They'd give Alan a story and a package to tell it

That flows nicely, I thought. I liked the Robin Hood bit.
You had to put the emphasis on the right syllables to make
it rhyme in time, but other than that, it had good flow.

I kept writing.

One day his boss came along with a cry
(A wondrous new product had entered the line).
'Alan, dear boy, I've something for you
This one kills EVERY insect. It's brilliant: all-new'
'Every insect?' asked Alan. 'That's rather a lot.
'Can I fit them all in? I've only eight spots.'
'Well, how many insects exist in this world?'
Asked the boss, whose brow was now somewhat furled.
'Well, there's flies and mosquitoes,' said Alan. 'Fleas and
*   moths.*
'Cockroaches, spiders and ants; that's the lot.'

'But that's only seven,' said the boss, thinking wrapping.
'We need one more creature or the artwork looks
*   lacking.'*
They paused for thought and both scratched their heads.
'Mice?' asked Alan. 'Does the stuff make them dead?'
'No, it's only for insects,' said the boss, looking
*   worried.*
'They need six to eight legs, and should preferably
*   scurry.'*
Alan gave in, and put his pen in its cradle
'I haven't seen anything else hiding under the table.'
'Nor have I,' said the boss. 'We're clean out of luck.
'Alan, dear boy . . . just make something up.'

Packaging was fun, and Alan liked to draw,
But he'd secretly been hoping one day he'd do more.
Here was his chance, a challenge divine;
It was time to create his own Frankenstein
And so Alan put his pen to paper
And started creating a creature with lasers
And guns, and venom, and daggers for claws:
An insect that killed things, breathed fire and roared.
'Goodness me, Alan, this thing will not do,'
Said the boss (he was frightened), 'it's all so brand new.
'Make something less scary, something less evil
'Or it'll never get past the marketing people.'

And so a new insect came to be born,
Without any poison or fangs or sharp thorns
The boss liked the roach head, and the long slinky lines,
'But now it's too harmless, can we give it some spines?'
Alan drew them, and then let out a wail,
He'd accidentally put the barbs on the tail.
The boss said he loved it. 'It's not a mistake!
'The public will buy it, it'll sell like hot cakes.
'The tail gives it purpose, a reason for hate.
'It'll make people kill it before it's too late.
'And in case they think they've only got mice,
'We'll say it eats paper and clothing and rice.
'Alan, dear boy, a name if you wish?'
Alan thought for a moment and said, 'Silverfish.'

Head office loved it and the packaging stuck.
The new insect helped them sell heaps of stuff.
Scientists questioned but never complained—

The creature looked common and normal and tame.
It was there on the label, and that was the proof.
No one was courageous to call out the spoof.
But I'd never seen one so I was suspicious;
I feared I'd been fooled by a plan quite malicious.
Of course I'd seen roaches, and spiders and flies,
But a silverfish never once passed my eyes.
I'd written it off as a ploy to sell spray
And figured the hoax would be over one day.
This creature was lunacy, I knew in my heart.
Because if it was real, we would have crossed paths.

But one sunny day on my white table-top
A small creepy insect ran out and stopped.
It looked quite familiar, like I'd seen it before
But not on a table, or carpet or floor.
And then I remembered the thing on the can
So off to the kitchen-sink cupboard I ran.
And sure enough, drawn near mosquitoes and flies
Was the six-legged creature I was meant to despise
I took aim with the spray and prepared for the kill
But I stopped 'fore the poison could make him
    feel ill.
He'd stood there with style, with grace and with
    pride:
Did he really need punishment with insecticide?
A slow painful death didn't sound like much fun
So I put down the can and I told him to run.
In a flick he was gone as his tail went swish-swish
That was the first, and last time, I saw a silverfish.

I put the pen down and read it back. It seemed OK. I called the waitress over. It was a Monday so she wasn't particularly busy.

'Hey, do you want to read the poem?' I asked.

'Sure!' she said.

I handed her the notebook. She sat down and read. It took her a couple of minutes. There were a few chuckles, which I took as a good sign. When she'd finished she looked up at me.

'It's great!' she said. 'I love it.'

'Really?'

'Yep.' She nodded. 'You're really good.'

I said thanks.

'I like your beard, by the way,' she said, smiling. 'It's cool.'

I blushed a little.

'Nice shirt too. My dad loves U2.'

CHAPTER 3
LOOK LIKE YOU'RE HOMELESS

It was Oscar Wilde who said that fashion is a form of ugliness so intolerable we have to alter it every six months. I like that quote. In Western cultures fashion changes quickly; it always has. For a long time I presumed that before the twentieth century people wore basically the same thing for a hundred years or so and then changed hairstyles whenever there was a revolution. Up until recently, my understanding of fashion history before 1900 had looked a little something like this:

1. Furry people
2. People wearing fur
3. Toga and sandals
4. Sack with belt
5. Hood with tights
6. Wigs and pointy hats

But it turns out fashion's journey through the ages has been a little more complicated than that. The Egyptians were wearing makeup before the first pyramids went up. The ancient Greeks made jewellery with more technical precision than NASA puts into the average space shuttle and the Romans liked clothes so much they invented the fashion parade.

And while the ancient cultures tended to find a style they liked and stuck with it, in the West we've always liked to mix it up. When early European explorers and traders started visiting the East, the cultures they found were alarmed at how often the new kids changed their style—they felt it suggested an instability and lack of order in Western civilisation. In 1609 the Japanese Shogun's secretary boasted to a Spanish visitor that Japanese clothing hadn't changed in over a thousand years; he also insinuated the pointy helmet the Spaniard was wearing was a little camp.

No matter how much our forefathers and foremothers liked to buy new hats, it was Oscar Wilde and his dandy friends who took things to a new level by elevating fashion hedonism to an art form. Oscar Wilde is famous for saying a whole bunch of insightful things, most of them about alcohol (another hipster staple), but his other famous fashion quote is that 'one should either be a work of art, or wear a work of art'. It's a philosophy that trendsetters have stuck to fervently ever since. And the works of art change every week.

Which was a bit of a problem for me.

Other than growing a beard and writing poetry, arguably the most important part of becoming the ultimate hipster was figuring out how to dress like the ultimate hipster. Nailing down precisely what the ultimate hipster should be wearing was going to be harder than nailing butter to a wall. (I was fairly certain U2 T-shirts didn't feature in the wardrobe though.)

I've always been reasonably fashion-conscious. I'm only aware of three major fashion crimes committed willingly and of my own accord. The first was as a thirteen-year-old in the early 1990s. My parents didn't believe in following fashion trends so we were only allowed to buy one brand-name item of clothing a year. I always chose an item of surfwear with as many tags on the inside as possible so I could cut them off and sew them onto garments my mum had made. I sported a pair of faux Billabong school shorts for almost three months before one of the other kids helpfully pointed out the fact I'd sewed the label on upside down.

The second transgression came the same year. We went on a family holiday to Fiji and Mum made us all matching purple parachute-silk tracksuits. From a distance we looked as if Prince had gone skydiving and landed haphazardly on the Armenian Special Olympics team. One day someone is going to find a photo of us and it's going to be put onto the internet and I am never going to have sex again.

The third came while I was at university. I was going through a gothic phase, so when I moved out of a rental house and in with my girlfriend I spent my entire $400 bond refund cheque on a pair of New Rock boots that had so many pieces of spiky metal on them they looked as if they'd been in a hand grenade accident. I still keep them in my closet in the hope that I can wear them to a retro goth fancy dress party at some stage in the future. I might also get drafted into the army one day and have to supply my own footwear, in which case I will be able to furiously kick my way into North Korea.

Since then though, my record has been relatively clear. I am by no means the most fashionable person on the planet, and I'm usually about three years behind what all the proper hipsters are wearing, but on the whole, I dress OK. Dressing OK obviously was no longer going to cut it.

I had two telephone calls to make. The first was to Lulu.

Lulu was an old friend of mine who works in the fashion industry. And by that I don't mean she works at a Target checkout, I mean she's one of the head buyers for an Italian clothing label. Lulu gets flown around Europe so she can attend fashion shows and make sure she knows what is cool.

Me: Hey Lulu, how are you?

Lulu: Good! I'm on a yacht.

Me: Awesome. There's a band called Yacht, they spell their name with a triangle instead of an 'a'.

Lulu: Triangles are cool. Very hipster.

Me: Are they fashionable?

Lulu: They're hipster fashionable.

Me: OK, I'll keep that in mind when I'm choosing shapes for my next gluten-free cookies. Hey, so I'm trying to find out how to find out what's cool before anyone else, in terms of fashion. How do I find out?

Lulu: I don't know, but when you do find out, tell me and you can be my personal assistant and I'll pay you lots of money.

I didn't believe that she didn't know. Surely it was her job to know. I asked her what her job was exactly.

Lulu: It's my job to like clothes.

Me: OK then. So how do you know which clothes to like?

Lulu: There are a handful of bloggers who decide and then everyone copies them.

Me: Really? Who are the bloggers?

She rattled off some names.

Me: And so, who *are* the bloggers? Are they the editors of *Vogue* and that sort of thing?

Lulu: No. One of them is a fourteen-year-old girl.

Me: Is that some sort of metaphor?

Lulu: No, she's a girl who has been alive for fourteen years. She started when she was thirteen.

Me: Are they all that young?

Lulu: No, one of them is seventeen.

Me: So how come they get to be the ones who decide what's cool?

Lulu: I don't know.

Me: Well, what gives them the power?

Lulu: They're just cool.

Me: That doesn't make any sense.

Lulu: I don't understand how it happens. People just take it as gospel. They all pretty much just like the same thing though. They all copy each other, but Karl Lagerfeld invites bloggers to his shows. They'll be there in the front row sitting next to the editor of *Vogue*.

This wasn't what I was expecting to hear. I was expecting to hear that there was a complex web of intrigue and sorcery and excitement and secret fashion shows and French designers running naked in Italian mountains.

On the flip side, keeping tabs on four blogs was going to be pretty easy.

Me: OK, so what's cool at the moment?

Lulu: We call it 'art garbage'.

She pronounced it 'gar-baahszj'.

Me: What is it?

Lulu: Well, it's basically a mixture of flannelette and Chanel. It's the art of looking homeless but being hip.

Me: They should call it Chanelette.

Lulu: That's good; you should be a writer.

Me: Why is it cool?

Lulu: Because everyone loves Kurt Cobain. And, in fact, if you look at all those blogs, you'll see it's basically what Courtney Love was wearing in the 1990s.

Me: Is grunge making a comeback?

Lulu: No, just the shirts.

Me: So are we just talking your standard flannelette shirt or is it just that pattern?

Lulu: No, it's flannelette. Only a bit thinner than what you'd see in a lumberjack shop. I don't know where everyone's getting their thin flannelette from, to be honest. Unless they're just washing it a lot.

Me: Is vintage still in?

Lulu: Not so much. Vintage will always be cool. A vintage Chanel dress will never go out of style, but vintage isn't necessarily cool any more.

Me: Are Ray-Bans still cool?

Lulu: Yes, but not with clear lenses.

Me: I was on Facebook before. There's a photo of you wearing Ray-Bans with clear lenses.

Lulu: When was the photo taken?

Me: Three years ago.

Lulu: Ugh. That's so embarrassing. Un-tag me.

Me: You must have thought it was cool at the time though.

Lulu: I don't want to talk about it.

Me: OK. Anything else I should know?

Lulu: Just look like you're homeless.

Me: OK.

This was an awfully good start. And being fashionable seemed pretty easy. All I had to do was read four blogs and sleep under a bridge.

I also now knew that Ray-Bans with non-prescription lenses were not only no longer cool, they had never really been very cool, and that their height of not even being very cool was so far in the distant fashion future they may as well have been Spandex. This was useful information.

I trusted Lulu's opinion but I wanted some more input. Lulu was hip all right, but her job was *being* cool. I wanted input from someone whose job it was to *tell other people* what was cool.

So I called Georgie.

Georgie was the deputy editor of possibly the most hipster magazine in the world and a former editor of the most hipster website in the world. We'd met through a bunch of music industry people we both knew, and when it came to knowing what to wear, do, and listen to, she was one of the prophets.

Me: Hey Georgie, how are you?

Georgie: Hey Matt, good. I'm dating a street artist at the moment and he had a show launch last night so I'm a bit hungover, but otherwise good.

Me: Where was the show launch?

Georgie: It was in an alley. It was raining so I've got a bit of a cold. Now I'm lying in bed with my flatmate's cat.

Me: It's twelve-forty pm on a Monday. How come you're lying in bed with a cat?

Georgie: It's working-from-bed day.

Me: So, I'm not saying you're a hipster in any way shape or form, but I want to chat to you about hipster culture.

Georgie: Oh, I'm a hipster. I don't deny the fact.

Me: Isn't the first rule of being a hipster *Don't admit to being a hipster*?

Georgie: Yeah. It's a stupid rule though. Every age has its cool kids. Hipsters will be the culture that the noughties are remembered for. In twenty years' time we'll look back and go 'noughties: hipsters', just like we do with the hippies in the 1960s, the New Romantics in the 80s and the grunge movement of the 90s. The irony is that hipsters try so hard to be hipsters it's stupid for them to not want to be called hipsters.

Me: So what fashion do you think typifies hipster culture?

Georgie: It has to be ironic, but I'm intrigued about how far irony can go.

Me: What do you mean?

Georgie: Wearing a biker T-shirt with wolves howling at the moon is cool. Wearing a Bon Jovi singlet to a party would be cool, but wearing a Nickelback shirt would be too much. Irony is a fine line. It's more than just clothes, though. Hipsters are all about throwbacks to bygone eras. They wish they'd lived when things were different. They love old Sega games, cartoons and comic books. They're apathetic and they don't trust the way the world is being run now. They're not negative, but if you don't like what's happening now and you're too apathetic to change anything or go to a rally the most you can do about it is write a song, and if you can't write a song, or a blog, you can at least bake some cupcakes—or better still, knit a scarf.

Me: So why is being creative such an important part of hipster culture and fashion, then?

Georgie: You could just go to an op shop and buy a knitted scarf—people used to do that. It was cool to find something no one else had. But creating it yourself is taking it a step further. If you can create something, that's cool. It's a way of saying to the world: 'Look at me, I'm contributing and I'm cool, value me.' It's all about perception.

Me: So is the most hipster thing I can wear a scarf that I made myself?

She thought about this for a while.

Georgie: Yes. No, wait. Yes. You could get plain black T-shirts and make band slogans with crazy glitter glue—that's cool, that's ironic—but a scarf is pretty cool too.

Me: OK.

Georgie: But it changes. Hipsters go through fashion cycles quicker than anyone. Things are only cool for five seconds. The only trend that won't die is clogs. But clogs are not cool. I wish that trend would die. You look like a fucking horse.

Me: So no clogs?

Georgie: No. No clogs. Learn to knit though. It'll pull the babes.

Me: Really?

Georgie: Yeah, chicks love a guy who can knit.

Me: OK.

I thanked her for her time and let her get back to her working-from-bed day.

This all seemed very easy. To be the most fashionable hipster on the planet all I needed to do was bake some cupcakes, read four blogs, find some designer flannelette and make a scarf.

Finding designer flannelette wasn't going to be too hard. I just needed to do some shopping at a cheap menswear store and run the shirts through my washing machine a few dozen times. I could probably even put some rocks in there to speed up the process. Cupcakes were also pretty simple. I could potentially even start a cooking blog while I was at it.

This craft thing was going to be interesting though. My memories of primary school woodwork are hazy, probably from all the glue I ingested at the time, but I do recall being so bad at it my that fingers, along with the Paddle-Pop-stick Christmas decoration I was making, ended up stuck to Erin Bowman's head.

Primary school was a long time ago though. My handicraft skills surely must have improved along with my general dexterity in the last twenty years. I could play guitar reasonably well; I could drive a manual car—how hard could knitting be?

CHAPTER 4
HIPKNIT

Haberdashery has long been one of my favourite words. It's up there with murmur, rural and periwinkle. It's such an old-world collection of letters, sprinkled with glitter and laced with charm. They don't make words like haberdashery anymore. In fact, they don't make haberdasheries anymore. Finding a craft shop in a major urban city in the twenty-first century is as easy as finding a knitting needle in a plastic haystack.

According to Google Maps, Nana's Nook was the closest old-school knitting retailer to my inner-city apartment, but it was 36.5 km away in the northern bayside suburbs—the kind of place where video stores still did a roaring trade, milkshakes were made with malt and, instead of shooting up heroin and burning wheely bins on Friday nights, teenagers engaged in wholesome activities like ten-pin bowling and youth group. You didn't get to that part of town on public transport: you called up Doc Brown and jumped in your Delorean.

Judging by the image on the homepage, the lady behind the counter at Nana's Nook could well have been Amish, which was retro-cool, but the shop may as well have been in Lancaster County, Pennsylvania. Its opening hours seemed to coincide only with nap time at the local nursing home too. If I was going to knit in a hurry, I'd have to make the trek south to the homemaker centre on the M1 instead.

Craft stores, like their hardware, furniture and electrical counterparts, have all been bought out by multinational corporations and moved to those giant warehouses in outer suburbs that have enough car-parking spaces to accommodate the gross domestic sports utility vehicle output of South Korea. It was wonderfully ironic that to mount a yesteryear revival and do something as beautifully kitsch and environmentally sustainable as knitting myself a scarf, I first had to mount a freeway and fight small four-wheel-drive automobiles for a park.

I had to buy a bookcase once, so I'd been to IKEA and had a vague idea how homemaker centres worked. On weekdays they were an empty warehouse wasteland. On Saturday mornings they became the amphitheatre of the suburban empire. In five thousand years when alien archaeologist anthropologists want to identify the point at which human society began to devolve, they will dig up a homemaker centre car park and find the skeletons of two thousand white lower-middle-class suburbanites, loading flat-screen televisions they can't afford into Hyundais they don't own, buried and perfectly preserved under a volcano of interest-free store credit paperwork.

Consumerism was a vicious downward spiral. If I was going to knit a ladder out of it I'd have to cop a Bunnings sausage sizzle on the chin for Team Hip. I had been thinking about turning vegetarian sooner or later, but hadn't given the butcher the finger just yet, so now was as good a time as any. It was time for a drive.

Finding the mega craft store was the easy bit. It's not easy to hide five million cubic feet of fabric, even if you are using a hardware store the size of Belgium and an IKEA you can see from space as camouflage. Nor was locating the knitting section an issue—I just used my phone's GPS to give me directions to the aisle. The problem was the overwhelming array of yarn to choose from. I didn't have the faintest idea what any of the gauges meant, and it all seemed to be pink.

I needed help. So I found a shop assistant. Her name was Beryl. Beryl had a moustache, but she seemed friendly so I explained that I was keen to get into knitting and needed help.

'Oh that's wonderful!' she said. 'You'll love it. Knitting is wonderful. Very therapeutic.'

'Oh good,' I said. 'Is it hard?'

'No! Not at all; the hardest thing is casting on.'

'Like in fishing?'

This confused her.

'Umm, no, well.' Her moustache twitched. 'Sort of, I guess. Casting on is when you do your first row of stitches. But you use a knitting needle instead of a fishing rod. And there's no bait. Or fish.'

'OK, good.' I smiled at her. 'I don't really like fish.'

Beryl said she didn't like fish either. 'They're a bit slimy,' she said. 'And I don't really like the sea. Too sandy.'

I told her I liked sushi though. She said she'd never tried it. We went off on a tangent about eating seaweed and the like. The consensus was that the best sushi for a beginner to try was something with chicken or avocado. Or better still, both.

'So, I was thinking of knitting a scarf to start off with, and then maybe progressing to something a little more interesting once I get the hang of it,' I said. 'What else can you knit?'

Beryl's eyes lit up at the thought. It was like asking a Mormon in for tea and explaining you were seeking a more personal relationship with Jesus.

'Oh goodness me,' she said. 'You can knit absolutely anything! Mittens, jumpers, socks—why, I even knitted a bikini the other week!'

I frowned a little at that. I looked her up and down and I think I may have also raised my left eyebrow slightly higher than my right.

'Oh, not for me, silly!' she said, sensing my worry. 'For my niece.'

This was good news. I hoped her niece had a better set of hedge trimmers than Beryl.

'Wasn't the bikini a little, well, see-through?' I asked. 'Most scarves and knitted things I've seen tend to have lots of holes in them. I would have thought holes and swimwear weren't a good match.'

'No, you use a really tight stitch and a small yarn,' Beryl replied. 'Like this.'

She pointed out some thin pink wool. I gave it a rub.

'It's not, ah, scratchy?' I asked, still doubtful. The only woollen garment I'd ever owned was my high-school jumper. It was as itchy as a hessian sack full of head lice.

If you didn't wear a long-sleeved shirt underneath it you were liable to end up with a rash. It also stank when it got wet in the rain. Not an ideal swimwear fabric, I would have thought.

'Hmm,' said Beryl. 'I didn't think about that.'

I nodded.

'So, I might start with a scarf and then see how I go,' I said.

Beryl thought this was a good idea. 'We sell the bikini pattern here if you're interested though,' she assured me. 'It's not too hard. Have you got a girlfriend? Or, or a boyfriend I mean. Whatever. Either is fine.'

I said I didn't have either at the moment, but that I'd just broken up with my girlfriend pretty recently.

She nodded.

I explained that since I broke up with my girlfriend I was trying out a whole bunch of new hobbies to see what I liked and that knitting was the third thing I'd started, after a beard and poetry. She thought this was 'marvellous'. Apparently knitting was becoming quite popular with the members of my generation. 'It's in all the magazines,' she said.

I nodded. She was a chatty one.

'So help me choose some yarn for a scarf then, Beryl.'

'What colours do you like?' she asked.

'Anything but pink.'

She thought that was wise. 'Pink will stain easily,' she said. 'How about blue?'

I didn't really like blue.

'How about black?' I said.

Black was the only colour wool they didn't have. I thought this was ironic. The black sheep were probably all hiding behind the shed smoking cigarettes when it was shearing time. Good on them.

We settled on a white yarn called 'Inca'. It was fifty per cent wool, thirty per cent acrylic and twenty per cent alpaca, which I thought was exotic. Beryl said it would make a fine scarf.

We then chose a pair of black 5 mm knitting needles and a crochet hook. I can't even remember what the crochet hook was supposed to do, but Beryl said it was essential so I let her put it in my basket. It came to $19.90 all up. As far as hobbies went, knitting was certainly cheaper than yachting. I waved goodbye to Beryl and she told me to come back and show me the scarf. I promised I would.

'Oh, and if you get stuck on anything . . .' she began.

I thought she was going to tell me to just give her a call.

'Go to YouTube. There's lots of tutorials on there.'

Owning haberdashery was one thing. Knowing what to do with it was quite another. I had no idea how to knit. Not a clue. I didn't even know what the needles did. I was presuming they worked a bit like chopsticks. My guess was that you put the yarn into a bowl and then magicked the needles through it and somehow a scarf appeared.

Suffice to say I was a little off track.

As promised, YouTube was full of how to knit videos. In fact, there were more knitting videos on the internet than there were films featuring naked cheerleaders. The knitting ones weren't nearly as exciting, but they were rather more informative. The stars weren't quite as good looking though. At least in the cheerleader videos only the male actors had moustaches. I was surprised Beryl didn't have her own channel.

I chose a video called 'How to Knit: The Basics' and settled in. It was only five minutes long and had a terrible royalty free techno soundtrack which I decided, for my own intents and purposes, to title 'Bush Doof '06: the Nanna Mix'. After the fifth run-through I realised learning to knit watching the internet is a little bit like learning to have sex watching porn—it looks fun when they do it on the screen, but try sticking a knitting needle in the same spot in real life and see how much fun you have. This wasn't going to work at all. I needed a coach.

'Claire?' I said, sticking my head through my flatmate's door. 'This is going to sound a bit weird, but you're a girl, and you're crafty: do you know how to knit?'

It wasn't as misogynous as it sounded. Claire grew up in Tasmania with a couple of hippie parents and she had quite a scarf collection of her own. She painted; she sang in a moderately successful folk-pop band; she was crafty. If anyone I knew was going to know how to knit, it was Claire.

'Is this for your hipster quest, or have you just completely given up trying to find a girlfriend?' she asked. 'Because I had a friend I was going to introduce you to. She's really cute, but if you want me to introduce you to my hairdresser David I can do that too. He's also really cute.'

I told her it was for my hipster quest thing and that I was thinking about buying a pet weasel, feeding it laxatives and locking it in her bedroom while she was away on tour with her band next week. I asked her if that would be OK.

She told me she could knit and that she would show me how if I bought her chocolate. We negotiated a fee of one block of Dairy Milk and I went to the shops.

'Knitting,' Claire said, 'is easy. Even for you. I know you're crap at handicraft, I've seen you trying to iron a shirt, but I think even you can learn to knit. There're only two things you need to know—casting on and off, and the knitting bit.'

I told her about my sushi conversation with Beryl. She thought that was funny. We ate some chocolate.

'OK, so do this.' She tied a knot around a knitting needle. 'I see you went for black knitting needles: nice. Very hip.' I said thank you. 'Then do this and this. And then this. And then that, see that, don't do this, do that—around here. And then do that again. And that's it. Repeat that until there are enough stitches on the needle for your scarf. The scarf will end up as wide as you make it here.'

It sounds complex when it's written down, but it wasn't too hard. She showed me a few more times and then I got the hang of it.

'Cool, now, that's the casting on bit, now you do the knitting bit.'

There was a similar set of instructions involving doing 'this' and 'that' and 'not here, but there'. It seemed easy enough. It didn't look much like a scarf at this stage. It just looked like a stick with some knots on it, but Claire assured me if I kept at it, I'd have a scarf in no time.

'How long is no time?' I asked. 'Like, twenty minutes? An hour?'

'How long do you want your scarf to be?' she said.

I told her I was hoping for scarf length, so maybe, I don't know. I went and got a store-bought non-hipster scarf from my wardrobe. It was about five feet long. I told her I wanted it to be as long as that.

'That'll probably take you a couple of weeks then.'

I swore.

'Maybe a week if you're really committed and you knit for a good few hours every day.'

No wonder nannas and hipsters were the only ones who bothered to knit anything. They didn't have quests to be on.

'What if I knit ALL day one day, for like, ten hours?'

Claire said that would probably just cut it.

'Why the hell do people knit then?' I asked. I held up the store-bought scarf. 'This only cost me ten bucks and it's super-warm and funky. That's a dollar an hour. My time is worth way more than that. How is it even economical to make a scarf then? Who works for a dollar an hour?'

'Where's your scarf made?' Claire said.

I looked. 'China,' I said.

And so I knitted. And I knitted. And I knitted. I knitted in the car at traffic lights. I knitted on the train. I knitted at picnics on grassy knolls, at cafés and at the shops. I even took my little hipster scarf project to a few little hipster gigs and stood up the back and knitted between sets. It got a lot of people talking.

Random strangers, many of them cute hipster girls, would see me knitting away randomly and come up for a chat. I was actually becoming known around my suburb as 'that hipster guy who knits'. I know this because one Sunday afternoon I was sitting in the park working away when a blonde girl wearing Ray Bans came up to me and said 'Hey, you're that hipster guy who knits.'

I wasn't sure if it was a compliment or not, but I was happy with the attention either way. The sun was kind of glinting in her eye and I thought I detected something of a twinkle.

'Ah, yep, that's me,' I said. 'I've just taken it up; it's kind of fun I guess.'

'That's so cool!' She said. 'My friends and I have seen you around.' She motioned to a group of trendy young things drinking cider by a tree.

'I love that you're just happy to sit here and proudly knit in the park. I really admire that.'

I told her it was nothing—just a little scarf I was working on. I asked if she wanted a go.

'Really?' she exclaimed. 'I'd love a go. That's so cool.'

I showed her what to do and handed it over. She messed it up straight away and we had a bit of a laugh. We chatted for a little while longer and I felt like we were really hitting it off. She was definitely potential hipster girlfriend material. I was guessing she lived nearby too, which was a bonus. I was a bit sick of long-distance relationships.

'So, I have to head off,' she said eventually. 'But it was really lovely meeting you.' I said it was great meeting her too. There was a bit of an awkward pause and I was about to ask for her number when she started talking at the same time. We laughed.

'You go,' she said.

'No, you go! I said, what were you about to say?'

'Oh, well, I was wondering, and I know that this is a bit up-front and all, but, umm, do you think I could I get your phone number?'

I made a mental note to thank Georgie for putting me on to this whole knitting thing. There was a God after all, and he was a craft-loving fellow.

'Yeah,' she said. 'My friend Michael just broke up with his boyfriend and he needs to get out of the house and meet some new people. He's really crafty too. You'd be just his type.'

CHAPTER 5
HIPSTERNOMICS—
THE MARKET STALL
PART I

'Georgie.' I was sitting in a park, on the telephone, talking to my fashionista friend—the one who had told me to start knitting because it would pull chicks.

'I need a creative way of getting rid of a scarf. I don't want to burn it because it's taken me two weeks to knit, and I don't think it'll burn anyway because it's wool, and a little bit llama I think.'

She told me she saw a burning alpaca once, in Peru. Although she'd had a lot of cerveza the night before and it could have been a piñata. She wasn't sure.

'Alpaca! That's the one,' I said.

'What?'

I told her not to worry.

'This is for the book, right?' she asked. 'Why don't you use it as a bungee cord?'

I told her that I had made it myself and that I wouldn't trust it not to unravel if I breathed too heavily on it, let alone used it to hang from a bridge.

'Give it to charity.'

I told her I'd said creative.

She thought about it some more.

'Can you turn it into an artwork?' she quizzed. 'Some sort of comment on the industrialisation of fashion?'

I thought this had merit. 'Maybe I could use it to create a sculpture of an orphaned Chinese sweatshop worker. How ironic would that be? It's a filthy hot sweatshop, but the kid needs a scarf.'

'Hmm.'

'No, wait, I could turn it into a noose. The kid could have hanged himself with a scarf because hipster culture has revitalised homemade craft and now society doesn't need mass-produced Chinese sweatshop goods any more. What do you think?'

Georgie told me it sounded like I was post-rationalising.

'Why don't you set up a hipster market stall and sell it?' she suggested.

I thought about this.

'Well, I like that idea, but it's not going to be a very big stall, is it? I can't set up a stall with half a scarf.'

We both agreed that wasn't the best idea. Then Georgie piped up.

'Why don't you go and get a whole *bunch* of crafty things, then? Make some jewellery out of board-game pieces—all the cool kids are doing that. Find some vintage clothes, write things on them in marker pen, bake some cupcakes, grow some organic vegetables, set up the ultimate hipster market stall and you can sell your scarf there.'

That, I thought, is a marvellous idea. I told her so, and hung up. She had possibly redeemed herself.

Every hipster neighbourhood in the world contained at least one organic vintage clothing craft market. Most reputable hipsterhoods sported a number of them. I personally couldn't walk outside my house on a Saturday morning without tripping over some dreadlocked communist selling hand-crocheted organic corn-holding mittens.

Their rise in popularity can be attributed to two things:

- The growing number of hippies who are nearing retirement age and have realised they have no life savings or superannuation off which to live, and so must quickly raise as much money as possible by cashing in on the only two things they know how to do:

  ~ grow organic vegetables
  ~ make homemade craft jewellery

- The growing number of hipsters with fashionable skin allergies who find themselves unable to digest anything but organic vegetables or wear anything but homemade craft jewellery.

I'd presumed hippies and hipsters had nothing in common but three letters and some beatnik history, but the more I thought about it, the more it became obvious that markets were the missing link. And if hippies were the most anti-capitalist sub-culture on the planet, the fact that they could find enough economic nous to rustle up stalls meant I should be a shoo-in. In fact, I figured I would most likely have market organisers begging me to set up shop with them. All I had to do was get some stock together and pick a Saturday.

Or so I thought.

As it turned out, market stalls were a little harder to get than I'd realised.

There were three main markets near enough to my house. A farmers' market that only sold organic produce and no craft, a craft market, and a giant 'everything' market that sold anything, as long as it was organic or crafty.

I wanted to properly cover all my hipster bases by selling both craft and organic food, so I sent off an application to the 'everything' market first. I had to download a form from the internet and answer a bunch of questions. The first and most pressing one was: 'What do you propose to sell?'

I hadn't really thought about that. 'Hipster stuff' wasn't really going to cut it. So I wrote:

'A fabulous selection of organic produce and handmade jewellery.'

The next question was: 'Do you manufacture your own products?' I said yes—that was the plan anyway. I wasn't sure precisely what yet, but I was thinking jewellery made from Scrabble tiles would make up a considerable section of my stall. They also wanted to know if I was certified organic, to which I said 'define certified', and whether or not I had public liability insurance. I had about as much public liability insurance as Osama Bin Laden but I ticked the yes box anyway and made up a fake policy number, figuring I'd get that sorted when they approved my stall. They also wanted some pictures of my merchandise, so I uploaded some tomatoes and a Scrabble board. It was unorthodox but I figured they'd be smart enough to see the value and give me a shady spot right by the chatty man with some macadamia nuts and we could exchange witty banter all day and he'd give me nuts.

Two weeks later I got back a reply from the organisers. They'd addressed it to 'undisclosed recipients', which was cause for some concern. I wasn't a big writer of official market correspondence myself, but I guessed that meant they might not have been as enthused about my stall as I was hoping. The letter read:

Dear Applicant,

Thank you for your application for a stall at the Davies Park Market, West End.

Unfortunately your application has not been successful.

Your application was considered carefully by us. Your product may not have satisfied our product eligibility criteria or, alternatively, it may not have been selected due to the competitive nature of the selection process. Due to the very high demand and the limited number of stalls available we have restricted the number of successful applicants in various product categories.

Thank you for your interest in the Davies Park Market, West End.

Kind regards,
All the team at the Davies Park Market, West End

This was not what I was expecting to hear. They sure liked to repeat the name of the markets though.

I put the failure of the application to the everything market down to inexperience and tried again at the craft market. This time I was more crafty. I went into a lot more detail about the products and included pictures of scrabble jewellery to give a better visual representation. I also told them that in addition to all the wonderful craft I would be selling I would also have a fantastic array of organic produce on offer. I made a private bet with myself that it was the best application they would have ever seen. I doubted anyone before me had the foresight to include an array of organic produce on their craft stall before. I thought it was genius.

They, apparently, did not. A man named Josh sent me this reply:

> The Valley markets do not allow any food products to be sold by stallholders. The types of products sold at the markets are clothing, accessories, jewellery, crafts etc.
>
> Thanks
>
> Josh Dargusch
> Valley Markets Co-ordinator
> Brisbane City Council

This was not going at all well.

With my first and second choice now out of the question I was going to have to aim for the farmers' market and try and smuggle in a little bit of craft without telling anyone. The only problem was, I didn't really have access to a whole lot of organic produce. There was some basil in my garden, and two rosemary bushes, but that wasn't anywhere near enough to fill a stall.

I put the call out on Twitter and Facebook to see if any friends nearby had vege gardens and all I got were some lukewarm offers of basil and mint. That wasn't going to do either. Hipsters ate more than herbs. I'd been reading a book on stuff white people liked and it said heirloom tomatoes were pretty much the ultimate hipster foodstuff. They were imperfect, organic and unable to be bought in a supermarket.

You also had to grow them yourself, which made them cool. If I was going to have the ultimate hipster market stall I was going to need the biggest, brightest, bestest, most heirloom organic tomatoes in the world. I wasn't sure exactly what heirloom tomatoes were, but I figured if they were given to me by my parents that would probably suffice. Luckily they had a vege garden. I was almost certain it had tomatoes in it too. I gave Mum a call.

Me: Hey, Mum.

Mum: Hello Matthew.

Me: Hey, what are you doing?

Mum: I'm doing the dishes. What are you doing?

Me: I'm trying to set up a market stall.

Mum: A what?

Me: A market stall.

Mum: At a market?

Me: Yes.

Mum: Why?

Me: It's a long story, but I'm not having much luck.

Mum: OK.

Me: Hey, what's in your veggie garden at the moment?

Mum: There're some weeds.

Me: By 'weeds' do you mean heirloom tomatoes?

Mum: No, by 'weeds' I mean weeds. There might be some basil. Do you want any basil?

Me: OK. Are you sure there are no heirloom tomatoes?

Mum: What's an heirloom tomato?

Me: I don't really know.

Mum: OK.

Me: Can you ask Dad if there're any tomatoes?

Mum: There aren't any tomatoes.

Me: What about pumpkin?

Mum: There's no pumpkin.

Me: But you guys always have heaps of stuff. What happened to your veggie garden?

Mum: Do you remember how we had a big flood up here and it rained a lot and everything flooded and people died and there was a flood?

Me: Yes

Mum: Right, well that's what happened. There was a flood.

Me: I see. So no veggies.

Mum: No. Just basil. Do you want some basil? I can give you some basil.

Me: I'm OK for basil.

Mum: OK.

Me: Thanks though.

Mum: When are you coming up next?

Me: I'm not sure.

Mum: Have you heard from Hipster Radio Station Ex-Girlfriend?

Me: No. I haven't heard from Hipster Radio Station Ex-Girlfriend.

Mum: She was nice. Find another girl like her.

Me: Yes, I know.

Mum: OK, sorry.

Me: OK, I have to go. Thanks though, love you.

Mum: Love you too. Be good.

Me: Bye.

Mum: Bye.

And that was that. No tomatoes. I was either going to have to set up a basil stall or find another supplier. I had no clue where to start looking. But then I had an idea.

A week or so earlier I'd been shopping at my local supermarket and had a bunch of vine ripened organic tomatoes in my basket. Vine ripened organic tomatoes were $14.99 a kilo, which was a bit expensive I thought. I'd finished up my shopping and was using the self-help checkout counter when it came time to put the tomatoes through. On the first page of the checkout screen they had a list of favourite fruit and vegetables you could pick from so you didn't have to scroll through the entire list to find what you wanted. Tomatoes were on the list. They weren't vine-ripened organic tomatoes though, they were just the normal ones. And they were $3.48 a kilo. A fifth of the price.

I was about to scroll through the extensive A–Z list of fresh produce to find vine ripened organic tomatoes, but I didn't know if they'd be under 'T' for 'Tomatoes', 'V' for 'Vine Ripened' or 'O' for 'Organic'. I suspected it would have been 'T' but I wasn't sure.

I knew if I scrolled through it would have taken me an extra ten to fifteen seconds and I was in a hurry to get home to finish the classic Hemingway novel I'd started reading. There were more than three hundred fresh produce items on the list, after all; scrolling would cut into valuable reading time.

It was at that point a little person inside my head, let's call him Satan, said:

'Hey, Matt, just pretend they're normal tomatoes and you'll save money and time. No one will ever know. They'll look the same when they're in the bag anyway.'

So I did.

I put them through as normal tomatoes.

But then I felt guilty. Really guilty. I was considering explaining my 'mistake' to someone in charge, but I decided they'd think I was an idiot. I got in the car and felt even more guilty about it, such were the moral values my mother had impressed upon me as a child, so I drove home and made a mental note to make atonement.

The next time I was at the supermarket I bought five normal tomatoes and put them through as vine-ripened organic tomatoes. I felt so much better.

But the incident now had me thinking. What if, instead of hunting around trying to find proper heirloom tomatoes, I just bought some of the ugliest looking vine ripened organic ones from the supermarket, poked a few 'authentic' insect holes in them and passed them off as heirloom tomatoes? It would technically be false advertising, but I could get around the karma police by selling the tomatoes for less than they cost me and giving away something else with every tomato purchase—a bunch of basil, for example. It would work sort of like a karma trading scheme—all the bad karma I would get by selling supermarket tomatoes would be offset by the price reduction and the gift. I could even give the proceeds to a charity which fed the homeless. That should be more than enough to cover the bad vibe deficit. It was so daring it just might work.

There was no online application for the farmers'

markets—the organisers were probably too busy in the fields to update a website—so I gave them a call. It took a while for them to answer but eventually a man, let's call him Barry, came on the line.

Barry: Yep.

Me: Hello? Is this the farmers' markets?

Barry: Yep.

Me: Oh good, I was wondering if I could get a stall?

Barry: Ah.

There was a pause. A longish pause. Long enough, I judged, for Barry to look around the room he was in, scratch his bottom and purse his lips thoughtfully. I could hear a TV in a background.

Me: Hello?

Barry: Yep. I'll just have to get Norma for you.

Me: OK.

Barry went away to get Norma. They were watching *Deal or No Deal*. I could hear Norma in the background, chastising someone for not taking the bank offer. Barry explained to her that there was someone on the phone asking about a market stall. She took a while to figure out what he meant, but she eventually came to the phone.

Norma: Hello, dear?

Me: Oh yes, hello, I was hoping to get a market stall.

Norma: Oh yes dear, well, we're very busy at the moment. There's none this week, or next week. The next spot I've got is, let me see, it's in a month, dear. But I usually reserve that for Brian the pumpkin man. He comes down on the third Saturday of every month, but his back has been playing up a bit so I don't know if he'll be able to make it. He has to come down from Bundaberg and his back doesn't like the drive, you see. That highway has more potholes than the moon. I can take your details if there's a cancellation though.

Me: Oh, OK, well, that sounds all right then.

Norma: What do you sell, dear?

Me: Well, I've got lots of herbs. Basil.

Norma: Oh yes. Laura is our basil lady, she's in stall 76.

Me: Ah, OK.

Norma: But we can always use more basil. Especially this time of year. It's hard to come by. Are you a grower?

Me: Ah, yes. Of sorts.

Norma: What do you mean 'of sorts', dear?

Me: Well, I grow a bit myself and I source organic basil from a few other suppliers. A bit like a co-operative, I guess.

Norma: Oh I see. Good. Good that you're all sticking together.

Me: Yes. I have tomatoes too. Heirloom tomatoes.

Norma: Oh really! Well, that's wonderful. Where are they from?

Me: Coles.

Norma: I beg your pardon?

Me: I mean, Coles Farm. It's a boutique growery near Toowoomba. They were hit by the floods though, you see, so I have to source from a range of suppliers.

Norma: A growery?

I coughed a little bit. I think she was onto me.

Me: Yes, that's what Joe calls it. Farmer Joe: he's a bit eccentric. Drinks a lot. Doesn't like to think of himself as a farmer, he's a grower. Says brewers run breweries, and he's a grower, so he runs a growery.

She seemed to buy that. We chatted about the floods for a while. I asked if they'd been bad for business and she said it hadn't been too bad. If anything they had been good for business because the major commercial market that supplies the supermarkets had gone under and most of the market gardeners had come through OK.

Norma: Anyway dear, my show is nearly on, but give me your details and I'll give you a call if something comes up.

Me: OK, thanks, Norma. What are the chances of something coming up do you think?

Norma: Well, someone usually drops out. You'll be fifth on the waiting list though, so, not very good to be honest.

Me: I see.

I thanked Norma again and let her get back to her show. This wasn't looking good at all.

I weighed up my options. I could set up a market stall on the street in front of my house I supposed. Sort of a garage sale with organic veggies. Or I could head out into the country and find a less in-demand market, but that wouldn't be very hipster. I really needed something a bit closer to home.

I called a friend who knew all the markets in the city and I offered to take her out for a drink in return for picking her brain. I suggested a bar in the funky part of town which served nine kinds of pear cider and she agreed. We met up for lunch.

Her first three suggestions were the three I'd already tried. She mentioned a few in other parts of the city but we decided they were for actual nannas who liked baby clothes, as opposed to hipsters who liked their nannas' vintage clothes.

Things were looking glum. We downed another couple of ciders and chatted about op-shopping for a while. We had a debate about whether tight jeans were still cool or not. We decided they were, but probably not for much longer. We felt that beige chinos were probably on the verge of making an ironic comeback.

It was still very early in the evening so the bar was almost empty. One of the staff trundled over to pick up our empty glasses and decided he was keen for a bit of a chat. We explained our dilemma. The bar was in a laneway and I joked that it would be the perfect place for a vintage clothing and organic produce market.

'Are you kidding?' the bar guy asked.

'No, look at it—it's the perfect set-up for a market. Shady, there's pear cider on tap and all the hipsters in town hang out here.'

'Yeah, we know,' the bar guy said, and disappeared cryptically back to the bar for a second.

He came back with a flyer.

'This Sunday,' he said. 'It's the second ever Curbside Craft Market. It's vintage clothing and craft. The boss is putting them on the first Sunday of every month from now on. We did one last month and it was a roaring success.'

This was too good to be true.

'How do I get a stall?' I asked.

'They're all gone, I think. But you can try contacting Ainsley here: she's running it. I'll give you her e-mail address. I'm sure you could bribe her. She loves cupcakes. Better be quick though.'

I bid my friend adieu, ran home to the computer and pumped out an email.

```
-------- Original Message --------
Subject: Re: Curbside Market Stall this weekend
From: Matt Granfield
To: Ainsley

Hi Ainsley, the bar staff told me to drop you a line.

A friend of mine is a fashion buyer for an Australian
importer and it's her job to go to Europe and buy amazing
clothes. She's got a massive personal collection and
she's keen to sell off some items quite cheaply. I've
also been put in charge of selling off a jewellery
collection belonging to a great aunt. There's some
amazing cool/kitsch/cheap stuff there. We'd really love
to have a small stall on Sunday at Kerbside if we can.

I know it's short notice, but we're willing to pay extra
if that helps and bribe you with organic cupcakes.

We'd only need a little stall and would be happy tucked
away in a corner. What are our chances?

:)

Matt
```

I was kicking myself for not getting her phone number. I should have just called. Who knows how long it could take for a hipster stall organiser to reply to an e-mail? If she was anything like the farmers' market people I would have been better off sending a carrier pigeon.

Luckily Ainsley was a little more tech-savvy than that. Within ten minutes she hit me back.

```
-------- Original Message --------
Subject: RE: Curbside Market Stall this weekend
From: Ainsley
To: Matt Granfield

Hi Matt,

Spaces are technically all supposed to be taken but
that jewellery collection sounds amazing so I'm sure we
can fit you in somewhere—I can't wait to see it actually.
I love vintage jewellery so I'll be going through it
with a fine-tooth comb. I'll see you on Sunday! It'll
be $25 for the day.

Kind regards,

Ainsley

P.S. Make the cupcakes raspberry ☺
```

*Sent from my iPhone so please excuse me if this message
looked like it was typed by a monkey wearing mittens.*

Now I was really in trouble. It was Thursday. I didn't have a great aunt, let alone a great aunt's jewellery collection. I had two days to find one or the other. Preferably the latter. I'd heard stories about great aunts. They made you kiss them on their hairy moles at family reunions. I didn't want that at all. I did have a market stall though, and a big dollop of chutzpah. That was a bonus.

I'd made up the story about the aunt thinking it would be a sure-fire way to get myself a stall at short notice. I was right. I hadn't made up the part about the friend who was a fashion buyer, of course. I just had to hope Lulu was free. Lulu was never free. I sent her a text message anyway, just in case.

Hey, do you want 2 run a stall in Brisbane with me on Sunday? I'm selling craft and organic veggies, you could just sell clothes. Just a few.

She wrote back within seconds.

This Sunday?

I confirmed it.

This Sunday! Got anything you want to sell?

I was pushing my luck and I knew it. Last I'd heard she was in London.
She replied though.

This sounds like fun!!! Count me in!!

The market gods were smiling on me. Lulu had more shoes than Imelda Marcos. At least I could count on her to bulk out the store with cool vintage clothes and I wouldn't be an idiot trying to sell half a scarf. All I had to do now was put together a vintage jewellery collection, make some craft and bake some cupcakes.

I also needed to get myself some new threads. I was still wearing the U2 T-shirt on washing days. It was time to go shopping.

CHAPTER 6
HIPSTER SHOPPING

'Mate, those jeans are tight.' This was my friend Ian talking. He's an accountant. His idea of outlandish fashion is waiting until Rivers has a sale and choosing the red socks.

'They're not really,' I said. This was a few months earlier and we'd been having a few drinks at his house before heading out for the night. I was playing DJ. Someone had made a joke about Michael Jackson and I'd just put on *Thriller*, so I demonstrated how not tight my jeans were by pulling some Billy Jean dance moves, followed by a series of brisk squats. 'See?'

Ian rubbed his goatee.

'No. No, they're tight. They're so tight that not only can I tell you have a phone in your pocket, but I can tell it's an iPhone. And not only can I tell it's an iPhone, I can tell what model iPhone it is.'

'That's not an iPhone in my pocket,' I replied. 'I'm just very happy to see you.'

'Well in that case, I think your penis is ringing.' He dialled my number to prove a point.

The man was right. I did wear tight pants. And tight pants were still very in. From the waist down I was already the ultimate hipster. I had the glasses too. Non-prescription Ray-Bans had been out of vogue for ages, but alternative thick-rimmed spectacles were still cool if you needed them to read, and I did. Tick.

I was lacking in every other department though. I didn't have the ultimate hipster shoes, shirts, socks, jewellery or haircut. It's not that my clothes were unfashionable — they were cool enough — they just weren't as cool as they could be.

There wasn't much I could do about the haircut. I was only thirty, but my locks had been thinning since I was twenty-five and it had been a year since I'd decided to go the shave and rock out in a number two buzz cut. I had a beard now, of course, but that was the best I could do up top.

The rest of my frame was a blank canvas. I figured I might as well start at the bottom and work my way up. My usual selection of footwear consisted of a couple of pairs of wicked vintage boots and a pile of Converse sneakers. While they were all pretty hip, I was about two years out of date and a true hipster would spot me as fraud within seconds. I really needed to get more current, so I called some friends, got a consensus on the hippest shoe store in the city and made my way over. It was primarily a sneaker store, but they apparently had some other cool stuff as well.

It was a Saturday afternoon but the shop was empty. I didn't know if that was a good or a bad sign. I guessed it was good from the perspective that no one else seemed to have heard of it, so it definitely wasn't mainstream, but bad in the sense that if these shoes were so cutting-edge hipster, only the most cutting-edge hipsters would realise how cool

Pre-hipster quest and looking not entirely un-hip, but certainly a long way to go.

Looking for poetry inspiration in a hipster café at the beginning of the quest.

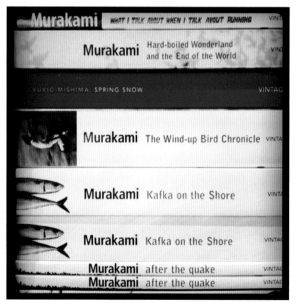

Haruki Murakami is widely considered the world's greatest living hipster author. I was in no danger of challenging him for the title.

Op-shopping for the ultimate flannelette shirt.

I love how this shirt not only has a triangle logo and a triangle tag, but instead of a date it has the phrase 'never established'. So unbelievably *alt*.

Fortitude Valley is undeniably the hipster capital of Queensland.

My new hobby became the ultimate babe magnet, just not in the way I imagined.

Red wine and Ernest Hemingway— part of a well rounded hipster diet.

I still don't really know why Scrabble rings are so hip, but they can be found at alternative markets and kitsch clothing stores all over the world.

Hipsters aren't known for their economic prowess, but running a second-hand clothing and handmade craft market stall is a rite of passage.

The elusive heirloom tomatoes. Number one on the list of foodstuffs hipsters like.

I never did manage to sell my unfinished scarf. It's still sitting in the cupboard.

Unfinished scarf. Suit hipster. Ready to go for winter. $10.00

Hipsters only need one gear to get cranking.

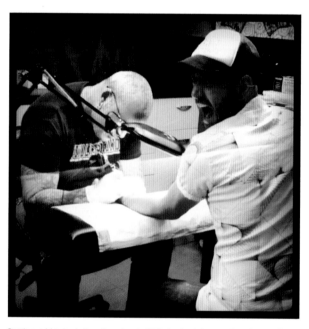

Getting a hipster tattoo. I pretended this hurt a lot more than it actually did.

they were. I decided the best thing to do would be to ask for help. These were the experts after all.

The shop assistant didn't look very hip though. He looked like he'd just walked out of a Run DMC video. And he had just switched the radio to a commercial FM station. I started freaking out, thinking maybe tracksuits and commercial radio was now suddenly cool, but then he apologised for the music saying that he was the owner of the store, the other two staff had called in sick and that the radio was broken and he couldn't work out how to use it. I let out a sigh of relief. He wasn't cooler than me at all. He was just a forty-year-old sneaker fan. Although I don't know if that made him hip or just a paedophile.

'Hey,' I said. 'I'm looking for some new kicks. What do you think are the most hipster shoes here?'

'The what?' he said.

'The most hipster shoes here.' I said.

He looked confused. Like I'd just asked him where he kept the potatoes.

'Hipster, like, what are all the cool kids wearing? What have you been selling lots of lately?'

He nodded. 'I like these,' he said, and walked me over to some vintage-looking green Onitsuka Tigers.

They were nice, but they weren't hipster. He had on the same pair. That was a bad sign.

'Have you been selling lots of these?' I asked.

He thought for a moment. 'No, not really, I guess. They're cool though, aren't they?' I agreed they were pretty cool.

'What's the latest sort of fashion?' I asked.

I already knew. I'd been doing my research. I'd been

watching YouTube videos of every buzz band in the world and they were all, at that point, wearing Vans sneakers.

He took me over to the Vans section. This was more promising.

'These red and black ones would look good on you,' he said, holding up a pair.

They were maroon. Sneaker Pimp was colour-blind.

'I'm not sure that's my colour,' I said. 'Have you got any in blue? I wear a lot of blue shoes.'

He thought for a minute and then went out the back.

'I've got these,' he said, holding up a pair of dark-green Vans.

'Umm. Maybe more blue than that?'

He went out the back again and came back with another pair. They were two-tone. One of the tones was the colour of the sea. The other tone was the colour of the sky. Bingo.

I took them. Tick. He even threw in a canvas bicycle-messenger bag with the store logo on it for free.

Next on the list was flannelette.

I don't know why flannelette was cool. Lulu had said it was because everyone loved Kurt Cobain, but grunge wasn't yet making a comeback in music circles. Perhaps it was an anti-fashion thing. Flannelette originated in Wales as a warm cloth for making sheets and shirts. At some point North American lumberjacks took it over, passed it on to Seattle musicians and there, I thought, it had died in the late 1990s. But it was back with a vengeance. I had to find me some.

I figured the best place to purchase flannel would be a fancy-pants hipster fashion store. I knew of one, hidden down a different lane near Fortitude Valley. I made the trek.

Sure enough, they had flannelette shirts in all shapes and sizes, but the prices seemed to be missing. I grabbed a black-and-white number from the rack in my size and took it to the counter.

The shop assistant was at least fifteen years old. Possibly sixteen. She was wearing a dress my ninety-year-old grandmother would have liked and a white belt my fourth-grade karate teacher would have loved. She had a tattoo of a dragon covering her entire right arm.

'Hi,' I said, with my best nonchalant hipster smile, trying to divert her attention away from the computer she was using. 'How much is this?'

She looked at me from her stool behind the counter, annoyed I'd distracted her from Facebook.

'A hundred and sixty dollars,' she said.

I walked around in a little circle—back to the rack, and then back to her. I must have misheard.

'I'm sorry. I thought you just said a hundred and sixty dollars,' I said.

This confused the little rabbit.

'Oh, umm, I did, it's a hundred and sixty dollars.'

This confused *me*.

'It's a flannelette shirt,' I said.

She nodded. 'It'll be warm.'

'Is it pure flannelette, or are there endangered species woven in?' I looked at the shirt. 'Giant panda, perhaps.'

She shrugged.

I wasn't paying $160 for a flannelette shirt. They were less than $20 at those discount menswear stores frequented by delinquent former footballers and that price included $19 worth of irony. For $160 I could also buy the entire menswear section of a Salvation Army op shop and have a new hobo-chic outfit every day for a year. Actually, that wasn't such a bad idea.

I put the $160 shirt back on the rack to save the shop assistant the trouble of logging off and went to find a charity shop.

It didn't take long. Brisbane's Fortitude Valley is the sex shop and strip joint capital of Australia. There are more vibrators in the Valley than there are people. It's so full of homeless drug addicts the two Subway restaurants offer honey mustard methadone as a sauce option. Named after a migrant ship that meant courage in the face of adversity, Fortitude Valley was once a thriving retail district. Now the only companies to call it home are those either trading in boobs (sex shops, strip joints, seedy bars), broken dreams (op shops, methadone clinics, discount Asian two-dollar stores), or both (advertising agencies).

Breasts weren't on my shopping list that morning. Flannelette was. And I was in luck.

There are two kinds of people who buy their clothing in thrift stores—homeless persons and hipsters. It's not surprising then that the sartorial line between the two is becoming increasingly blurred. Hipsters used to go to op shops to find funky, one-of-a-kind scarves and random items of gorgeous vintage fashion. Now funky clothing store owners raid the clothing bins out the back in the wee hours of the morning before St Vincent de Paul staff can even get to them, sneakily stealing anything with aesthetic value and selling it for five times the original price in their retro inner-city boutiques. As a result, the only items left on op-shop shelves these days are garments that hobos—people who are so desperate to get high they will lick bleach off a footpath—have deemed not fashionable enough to be seen in.

And that included a little red-and-blue checked number made from one hundred per cent nylon flannel I picked up for $2 at Lifeline. Ironic T-shirts were also in abundance. I found a vintage 1990s Bart Simpson top for $3, an 'I visited Minnesota' souvenir shirt for $1.50, which featured a picture of a wolf, and the pièce de résistance—a white piece of Ed Hardy glitter glory for $4. The sixty-something-year-old man volunteering at the counter was as impressed as me.

'Ed Hardy,' he said, shaking his head in a disbelief I couldn't define as sarcastic or serious. 'How much would that have been new?'

I reckoned we'd have been looking in the vicinity of one to two hundred dollars.

Ed Hardy, if you don't know, was a Californian tattoo artist and designer who popularised sailor tattoo designs in the 1960s and 70s. He was brilliant. In 2004 a French fashion designer and entrepreneur named Christian Audigier (the man who invented the Von Dutch brand, subsequently brought back the trucker cap and created the world's first branded condoms) licensed Ed Hardy's imagery, bought two thousand tonnes of glitter and produced a range of T-shirts for cashed-up bogans who liked shiny things. They sold in enormous numbers in the western suburbs of the world's cities before the company went bankrupt after someone told the bogans how gay they looked in glitter. Fashion has not reached such a dizzying pinnacle of vomit-inducing gaudiness since. You would have to literally wear a hat made of drag queens to push the envelope any further.

Buying an Ed Hardy T-shirt in an op shop for $4 was as ironic as it was possible to be without opening up a wormhole in the theory of relativity and unexisting Yahoo Serious. I don't know if the man behind the counter realised this, or if he just thought I lived in a caravan with my mother, but he did think I had rather a bargain on my hands.

He shook his head. 'That's quite a saving.'

I nodded.

'Hey, have you got a change room or anything? I want to put this on.'

'Not really, but there's a toilet out the back. You can change there if you like.' He gave me the key.

I changed.

I came back to give him the key and then thought I'd try my luck a little further.

'Hey, you haven't got any board games, have you? Specifically, Scrabble. With wooden tiles.'

'Sorry. I've got Pictionary,' he said helpfully, motioning to a shelf which had an assortment of puzzles and some jigsaws with pictures of Europe on them.

'Hmm, no, I need Scrabble. What about jewellery?' I asked. 'Have you got any old jewellery?'

He pointed to a counter behind me. There were a few odds and ends, some rings and things, but nothing to get excited about.

'That's OK,' I said. I'd had enough luck in this shop for one day. There were plenty more. One of them had to have Scrabble.

As it turned out, either the homeless people of Fortitude Valley had a penchant for scoring triple words with their heroin and every op shop in town had sold out of the hipsters' favourite word game, or the street value of Scrabble was so high everyone was hanging onto their tiles for fear of a letter drought. Either way, it wasn't looking good. I went to every op shop in town and had no more luck. There was no vintage jewellery around either.

I decided to cast the net even wider and head to the larger charity warehouses in the outer suburbs. Nothing. I picked up a few more ironic T-shirts and some cassette tapes, to make tape necklaces as a back-up craft plan, but it wasn't the same.

I wanted to make Scrabble rings. Badly. I'd first seen them being sold at the Camden markets in London a few years earlier and since then they seemed to pop up everywhere I travelled—in Haight-Ashbury, Melbourne, Notting Hill and Glebe—but I'd never seen them in my home town. They were the ultimate expression of hipster craft—ironic, intellectual, artsy and homemade. I wanted to be the one to bring Scrabble rings to Brisbane.

The new board games were all made of plastic and the tiles weren't as cool, so it wasn't like I could just duck down to Toys 'R' Us and pick up a set. I needed the cool factor of wood. A few friends owned the game but from memory they all had the plastic version. The only place I'd seen locally which had an old-school board with wooden tiles was a hipster café down the road from my house called Cirque. I used to play friends there on Sunday mornings over a cup of tea and some corn cakes. But they were hardly going to just let me raid their games shelf.

I couldn't just rock up and walk out with the Scrabble board either. That was larceny. Nor was I about to just steal a few tiles. That wasn't cool. Some poor hipster in a few months' time would be stuck with a Q and the only U left in Brisbane would be on some indie Ursula's finger. A game would be lost over it and I didn't want that kind of karma on my head. When I thought about it, I could actually probably make do with just one letter. As long as I used the right amount of superglue and nailed it on the first attempt I should be fine.

All I had to do was get them to part with a tile.

I headed over, ordered a pot of tea and some corn cakes and planned my attack. They tried to seat me out the front but I asked if they had a table upstairs, where I knew they kept the board games.

I was in luck.

I figured the best, most honest, thing to do was find whichever letter was the most common and then offer to buy it from them. I got out the rule book and flipped through to the letter count. There were 100 tiles all up. E was the most common. I calculated that in a full Scrabble set there were twelve Es. Surely they could spare one. I counted all the letters in the bag and five were already missing anyway. It wasn't like taking one more would ruin the game for everyone. I put a letter in my pocket so I could ask about it at the counter when I went to pay the bill.

'Are you playing Scrabble?' A waitress suddenly appeared behind me. I almost jumped out of my chair.

'Umm, ah, yes. No, well, yes. I was just about to.' I said. I coughed nervously. She must have seen me take the tile. She had probably already called the police. I could see the headlines now: 'Hipster busted at trendy café with E in his pocket.' It was going to be very hard to explain this to Mum.

'Well, do you want a bigger table? This bench is pretty small, isn't it? You don't want the board falling off—we'll lose all our letters.'

'Oh there's plenty here still,' I said. 'I just counted: there are only five missing. I thought there'd be more gone, but there're ninety-five letters here. That's heaps, hey?'

She looked at me the same way the waitress looks at Dustin Hoffman in *Rain Man* when he counts the toothpicks.

'Right.'

I said I was OK at the bench and finished my corn cakes. They were rather delicious. I couldn't hide upstairs all day though, so I went downstairs to pay.

'That'll be $18.90,' the cashier said. It was time to make my move.

'Cool. Hey. Umm,' I brought the tile out of my pocket. 'I was wondering if I could buy this as well. Please. If that's possible.'

The cashier looked at me like I'd offered to sell her some Amway.

'No, I don't think so,' she said. 'Someone will need that.'

This wasn't the plan. I figured they'd have just given it to me for being so nice. I could have just stolen it and not told them.

'Actually, I counted the letters. There are already five missing, so it's not like you've got a perfect set.'

The cashier was now looking at me as if I'd just told her I'd taken some pictures of her son in the bath and was offering to put them on the internet for her.

'No.'

'What if I give you ten dollars?' I pulled a note out of my wallet.

Her supervisor came over. 'Is everything all right?' he asked.

'Hey,' I said. 'I was wondering if I could buy a Scrabble tile.'

'Why?' he asked. Suspicious. His was a pretty reasonable question.

I needed some sort of sob story about a dead sister's dying wish and how she wanted a letter E from her favourite café burned with her ashes and scattered in her favourite park, but nothing came to me.

'I want to make some jewellery out of it.' I said.

'I can't, I'm afraid,' the supervisor said. 'It's not mine to sell. The owners will be here next week though if you want to come in on Sunday. I'm sure they'd probably be happy to sell it to you then.'

'Ah,' I said. 'I kind of need it today.'

He shrugged. 'Sorry. Can't. Come back next week.'

Another waitress had overheard the conversation and chimed in. 'Hey, did you say you wanted to make jewellery out of it?' She asked.

'Mm.'

'Well, there's a place over the other side of town that sells the pieces. An antique shop. They're made into rings, but they have heaps of them and they're really cheap. You could just pull the Scrabble pieces off and make them into whatever you wanted to make them into.'

'I see.'

She nodded helpfully.

'Want me to write down the address for you?'

I said that would be most helpful. She scribbled something on a piece of paper. It wasn't far away at all. Just over the river in a part of town I'd never really spent much time in. I thanked her, paid the bill, left them a tip and headed over.

The place was exactly where she had said. It was one of those antique market things where people who collected junk all had stalls inside a large shitty warehouse in the wrong part of town. Right there on the counter was a box overflowing with Scrabble rings. I wasn't going to be the first hipster to bring Scrabble rings to Brisbane, but I was at least going to partly fulfil my hipster dream.

'How much are these?' I asked the girl behind the counter. She was dressed as a rockabilly—swallow tattoos, pony tail, quiff and a vintage dress. She was so cute I wanted to take her home.

'Ten dollars each,' she said with a wink. 'But I hope your name starts with U or I. All the good letters are gone, I'm afraid.'

I told her my name was Matt.

'Bad luck. Well, it's a nice name, but bad luck on the Scrabble ring front.'

I asked her name.

'Sally.'

'Damn,' I said. 'I could have bought you a ring. Now I guess we can't get married.'

She thought this was cute.

'Hey,' I said. 'You haven't got any old jewellery, have you?'

She looked at my Ed Hardy T-shirt. 'Well, I haven't got any thick gold chains, if that's what you're after.'

'I was thinking more along the lines of 50s kitsch.'

'You'll have to go and have a look,' she said. 'Stuff turns over all the time; just have a wander around.'

I did. There were some amazing, expensive heirloom pieces, and a few rings made from typewriter keys, but nothing I could afford. Nothing resembling a great aunt's collection. I was going to have to make up a story to Ainsley at the markets tomorrow. I figured I could tell her my cousin got to it before I did. I had plenty of other stuff to sell now anyway, so it wasn't like my stall was going to be empty. Still, it was a shame. Hipsters loved vintage jewellery. I wasn't really going to have the *ultimate* hipster market stall without it.

I admired some of the other wares for a while and then came back to the counter to buy a ring from Sally.

'How'd you go?' she asked.

I shrugged. 'There's some lovely stuff, but nothing I was really looking for.'

She pulled out a box from below the counter.

'I'd totally forgotten about this,' she said. 'I thought of it while you were gone. We found it in an old wardrobe someone brought in. It was just sitting in the bottom drawer.'

She put the box next to the register. It once would have contained a pair of shoes. The kind a rich, quirky nanna would have bought in the early 1970s.

'Came in earlier in the week. Someone's grandma died and they were getting rid of the furniture. There's nothing expensive in here, no gold or silver or precious jewels or anything—in fact it's mostly just tasteless crappy brooches and earrings from the 1950s and 60s—but you're welcome to have a look. I haven't put it out on display yet because it's all tangled up. We were going to just sell the items for a dollar each.'

I had never doubted the existence of God, but it was nice of him to prove himself like that from time to time. I couldn't have been happier if Mary-Louise Parker had turned up naked on my doorstep late one Friday night for sex practice.

The box was metaphorically, if not literally, a gold mine. It contained a set of old brooches with birds on them, numerous triangle earrings, some fake pearls, pendants, a couple of broken watches, twenty or so large rings which looked like they'd been stolen from Liberace's penthouse while he was doing the dishes and dozens of other little trinkets too numerous and kitsch to catalogue here.

I was beaming. Sally smiled back.

'How much for the whole box?' I asked.

She shrugged and peered in.

'Thirty dollars,' she said.

'I'll take it.'

All I had to do now was bake some cupcakes. Raspberries were in season, which was good. And I knew just where to find the organic flour in the health food aisle in Coles.

This was going to be the most hipster market stall ever.

CHAPTER 7
HIPSTERNOMICS—
THE MARKET STALL
PART II

I would totally be a morning person if the sun got up four hours later. As it was, the only way I would ever be happy rising at dawn was if I had a winter home in Sweden where first light is around 11.30 and it gets dark again just after lunch. That idea actually had appeal, too. Log cabins are very hipster indeed—other than a Moleskine notebook and an acoustic guitar, nothing goes better with a long, unkempt beard than a cabin in the woods.

In fact, the only thing stopping me having a winter home in Sweden was that fact that I couldn't ski or ride a snowmobile, so if I lived there I'd be stuck indoors for three months of the year. That kind of isolation would do wonders for my knitting career, but the only thing to eat in a Swedish log cabin in winter is pickled herrings and I wasn't a big fan. Pickled cucumber on a cheeseburger, yes; mad for it. Pickled fish in a jar, no. You already know my views on IKEA furniture.

So, not being a morning person in any way, shape or country, one of the things I'd been dreading most about running the ultimate hipster market stall was the part where I'd have to rise at four am, set up a tent and chat with hippies about the weather. I could happily chat to hippies about Bob Dylan at midnight after a few ciders, but chatting to hippies about the weather at dawn after no ciders was completely out of the question. Thankfully, the Curbside Craft people had been thoughtful enough to put their markets on, not only inside a bar, but at twelve noon—or as hipsters usually refer to it, beer o'clock.

Ainsley had suggested Lulu and I arrive at ten-thirty am to start setting up, but this seemed excessively early for a Sunday, so I decided to get there at eleven-fifteen. Lulu was late to every event, function and gathering I'd ever known her to attend so I told her to be there an hour earlier, figuring she'd get there about the same time as me. The rule I had with Lulu was to tell her to be wherever we had to be an hour before we actually had to be there so she'd turn up roughly on time. Even then, she didn't show up to the markets until eleven-forty-five. By which time I'd given Ainsley five organic raspberry cupcakes, eaten three myself, driven halfway across town and back to buy some packing boxes to set up our stuff on after I realised I didn't own a foldaway table, and had a fight with a homeless person who I thought was trying to steal stuff from the stall owner next to me, before I realised he *was* the stall owner next to me. He was selling clothes out of a couple of suitcases—five dollars an item or three for ten dollars.

When Lulu did finally arrive she was at least apologetic.

'Sorry,' she said. It was a bit of a hike from where she'd parked to the market and it was an uncharacteristically warm autumn day so she was a little dishevelled. 'I had to go to the beach.'

Lulu was one of my favourite people in the world because

she was the kind of person who would get up at ten am, know she had to be somewhere at ten-fifteen am and instead of rushing to be there on time, she would instead decide to go to the beach. As long as she never got a job in air traffic control, the world would probably continue on without her.

'It's alright,' I said. 'I'm pretty much done now anyway.'

Lulu put her bags down and had a look around. She nodded her approval. The stall looked good. The packing boxes had been covered with a couple of tablecloths to make a nice neat counter, the antique jewellery collection was gleaming and resplendent in the midday sun and the wall behind us was a latticework section backing on to part of the venue, so I'd been able to hang up featured clothing items like they did on the merch counter at a festival. I'd also managed to scrounge up a few vintage-looking items from my own wardrobe to go with the ironic T-shirts. I'd even grabbed an old guitar and some books to give it an arty feel. Pride of place was saved in the middle of the front row for the Scrabble ring and some tape necklaces I'd made myself that morning. I put them on the bicycle messenger bag the shoe store man had given me so they had a bit of a backdrop.

'Tape necklaces,' she said. 'Cool. Did you make them?'

Given that tapes already have two large holes in them and that all I'd done was thread a chain through the middle, 'made' was a pretty generous interpretation of my handiwork, but I said yes.

'I'll give you one if you like,' I offered. 'Do you want the Wham! single featuring "Wake Me Up Before You

Go-Go" or *The Best of Johnny Farnham: Johnny Farnham's Greatest Hits*? It was released before he'd really had any hits, which makes it pretty ironic.'

She thought about this.

'I've got the best of Europe too, and a couple of ones by John Denver,' I offered.

'Umm. I'm OK actually,' she said.

I nodded.

'Looks good though,' she said. 'You've done a great job. I'd better get cracking: can you give me a hand setting up my bit?'

She had about fifty items of clothing stuffed into a couple of suitcases and a rack on which to hang everything. Some of it was stuff she'd made herself; the rest was a random assortment of weirdness from around the world. Lots of it had glitter. My favourite piece was a jumpsuit which looked like it was made from autumn leaves. It had a tag on it that read $15. In fact, she had tags on everything. I hadn't thought as far ahead as that.

The other stall owners had all finished setting up and had started to mill around looking at things so I figured I'd better put some prices on things quick smart. Given that Lulu's job was working out what clothes were worth, I asked her to give me a hand.

I held up a vintage woollen waistcoat which I'd bought at an expensive antique clothing store in Melbourne a few years before for $100. It was made in England during the Second World War. I quite liked it and didn't really want to sell it, but I'd brought it along to pad out the store a little.

'Thirty bucks,' Lulu said.

'What?! I paid a hundred for it a couple of years ago and now it's even more vintage, so it should be worth more than that by now.'

'Did it have a large wine stain on it when you bought it?'

I admitted that it didn't.

I found a tag, reluctantly wrote '$30' on it and hung the waistcoat back up.

'What about this?' I asked. It was a tweed coat which I'd bought new, from Lulu's store, three years ago. Unlike the waistcoat it was in almost mint condition. I think I'd paid $300 for it. I thought it was pretty cool.

'Forty,' Lulu said.

'What! What's wrong with it?'

'Nothing,' Lulu said. 'It's just not in fashion.'

I scowled.

We got to the Ed Hardy T-shirt. She didn't know what to make of that. I insisted it was ironic. She wasn't so sure. 'It's too soon,' she said. I disagreed. She said it would act like hipster repellent for our stall—they'd see the glitter from miles away and run in the opposite direction. I said true hipsters would appreciate the fantastic irony.

'Put $2 on it and stick it up the back somewhere,' Lulu said.

I wouldn't budge. I wanted it on display and I wanted at least twenty bucks for it. Lulu insisted it wasn't ironic. So I called Georgie and explained the problem. She thought about it for a while.

'It's definitely ironic,' was her advice. 'But it's dangerous.

You need to do more. Turn it into something else so no one mistakes you for a bogan. Even if you've got an ironic moustache, a fixed gear bicycle and you're drinking a soy chai latte at the time, wearing an Ed Hardy T-shirt trumps all of that. It's like putting one red pair of socks in with all your white American Apparel deep-v-neck T-shirts — they're all going to get tainted and come out at least a little bit pink. Get a marker and write a band logo on it or something.'

I thought this was good advice. Lulu did too. I got out a Texta.

'What can I write?' I asked.

Lulu shrugged.

'It looks like someone has taken to it with a Bedazzler,' I said. 'You remember those? It was like a stapler that put sequin things on your clothes. They were really popular in the 90s.'

Lulu had no idea what I was talking about.

'I bet that's how they came up with the idea. Ed Hardy and his mates would have had a few beers and then sat around a table thinking, "How can we get our shirts to stand out from the crowd when it's dark? They're all bright in the day, but when it gets dark — nothing. Wait. I know, we'll Bedazzle them a bit." And that's what they did.'

She thought the idea had merit.

'Someone even had the idea of vajazzling too. I don't know if it was Ed Hardy, but it was definitely a thing.'

Lulu asked what vajazzling was. I explained it was like Bedazzling, but for, well, you know. Lulu thought this was amusing when I explained it didn't involve a stapler and that the vajazzles were self-adhesive or applied with skin-safe glue.

'What about I write "Ed Hardy school of vajazzling" on the shirt?'

She said no. No one would get it. 'It needs to be a bit more shocking.'

'What about "My c*** is vajazzled by Ed Hardy",' I suggested.

She thought that would be perfect. But that I'd better put it out of reach of small children or there were going to be some awkward questions from the Australian Christian Lobby.

I wrote it, hung it up high and put a $20 sign on it. It was art.

Next up was the flannelette shirt I'd bought for $2 at Lifeline. I insisted on charging $15 for it. 'They're $160 down the road,' I explained. 'This will walk off the shelves.'

Lulu felt that charging $15 for a shirt which cost me $2 was a tad excessive. So I wrote my name on it with a glitter pen and explained that it was now a designer flannelette shirt, and that the price was now $150; I didn't even need another tag, I just added a zero. I explained that that was how the fashion industry worked. She reluctantly accepted this.

I decided to make up some other more in-depth signs for some of the more interesting pieces of merchandise.

I'd bought some fake Ray-Bans from the craft market up the road for $10 each so they got a sign that read: 'Sunglasses: $15 each. No more squinting for you, hipster!'—I figured I'd better try to make a profit on something.

I created a special little stand for Johnny Farnham and wrote: 'Yes! You can own Johnny Farnham's seminal classic *Johnny Farnham's Greatest Hits* in tape necklace format. Tell your friends you liked him before *Whispering Jack*. Was $500, now only $10: bargain.'

In my op-shop travels I'd also found some old, unlabelled reel-to-reel tapes in the bottom of a box. I figured there was a small chance they were missing Beatles masters, so I wrote a sign for them that read, 'May or may not be lost Beatles tapes: FACT. $1 each or two for $5.' I expected them to sell quite quickly.

I had some old retro hats too. I'd worn them and they were a bit smelly so I decided that made them worth more. 'With these hats you could start a jazz band,' I wrote. '$35 each.'

The jewellery collection was priced off at $1 an item and I decided to ask $10 for the Scrabble ring. I put a sign on the cupcakes which said you could get one free with every purchase over $20.

The only thing left to price was my unfinished scarf. In the excitement of the previous day I'd completely forgotten about it. It was the whole reason I was here, after all.

'How much do you reckon for a scarf?' I asked Lulu.

She thought about this. 'Well, it's not really finished, is it. So that either makes it really valuable, because it's a piece of art, or it makes it completely worthless.'

I decided to put a sign on it that said 'Unfinished scarf. Suit hipster. Ready to go for winter: $10 (includes free knitting lesson).' It still had the knitting needles and ball of yarn attached, so I figured that was a pretty good deal.

Now all we had to do was wait for the customers to arrive.

We waited a while. Quite a while actually. The markets were technically open for business at midday, but it was twelve-thirty by the time we were ready and we'd been too busy pricing things to notice that there weren't actually any customers in the market. This was strange. They'd been advertising the thing on their Facebook page and handing out flyers in the bar for a while. Every hipster in town should have known it was on. The bar was open, but there was just no one around.

Lulu and I exchanged glances and shrugged.

I asked the homeless guy if he knew where everyone was.

'Yeah, it's the seafood and wine festival,' he said, and scratched his bum.

'What seafood and wine festival?' I asked.

'Over at Caxton Street. You know, the Caxton Street Seafood and Wine Festival.'

I said I didn't know.

'Yeah. On every year,' he said. 'All the cool kids go. No one's going to be here today.'

I asked him why he'd set up a stall if no one was going to be here. He said he would have been at the seafood and wine festival but he drank all his wine.

I decided to do some more knitting while we waited. I had a heated discussion with Lulu over whether or not knitting more of the scarf would add to or subtract from the price. The argument was inconclusive.

Finally, at one-forty-seven pm someone arrived. I know this, because I wrote the time down in my Moleskine notebook. It was a girl, aged about nineteen. She browsed for twenty seconds, and then went the homeless guy's stall. Another couple arrived a few minutes later, laughed at the hat sign and also moved on. I got excited at two-twelve when someone picked up a tape necklace, but they put it down again before trying it on. Lulu said not to worry.

I was hungry by then, so I decided to go find a sourdough sandwich. The bar didn't serve food, so I had to head up the road. Lulu said she'd watch the stall. We joked about her being able to cope. The guy at the sandwich store said he'd never seen a tape necklace before. I took it as a compliment, but I don't think he meant it as one.

When I got back Lulu was excited.

'You've had your first sale!' She cried.

'Really?'

'Yep.'

'What?'

It was some placemats I'd bought at a Chinese two-dollar shop. They had holograms of wolves howling at the moon on them. They changed position as you moved past. They were horrible, but horribly ironic. They'd cost me $3.50 each and I'd sold four of them for $15. I'd made a dollar.

'Better still,' Lulu added. 'The organiser girl came past

and she said the jewellery collection was rad and that we had the best stall.'

I pointed out the fact that the stall next to us was a homeless man.

'Yeah, but that guy over there is selling books and they're good books. We're beating him.'

We decided to have a cupcake to celebrate.

Lulu managed to get rid of a few dresses and things over the next little while, but it was another two hours until my next sale. I was feeling chatty and when a cute girl picked up a heart-shaped pendant that was covered in obviously plastic diamantes I joked that they were real. She didn't hear me so I said it a little louder. She asked what I'd said. It wasn't funny any more so I explained that I had just been joking that they were real, and, obviously, there weren't.

'I'm deaf,' she said. But in that deaf voice deaf people have, so it sounded like *Arm der*. 'Can you talk slower, please?' She was trying to read my lips.

'Oh,' I said. 'I'm. Sorry. I. Said "they are real". But. They are not. Real.'

She nodded and looked surprised. Surprised and gorgeous.

'They're real?'

I shook my head. This wasn't going well. The homeless man had overheard bits of the conversation and was looking at me now in disgust. I think he was about ready to step in and have a word.

'No. Not real.' I said. Shaking my head vigorously and mouthing the words. She finally got it.

'How much?'

I felt bad so I just told her to take it. She tried to give me $20, but that was way too much. It only cost me $10. In the end we settled on $10. I was happy with that. I was considering asking her out, but now she just thought I was weird.

I made one other sale before closing time. It was to a Russian woman who offered Lulu and me $12 for three necklaces. It was about five o'clock and neither of us could care less about the price. We just wanted to go to the bar. We'd tried to get ciders earlier only to be told that the lane we were in was a no-alcohol zone. She wouldn't leave though. She kept asking the price of everything. I told her the scarf was now $100 and she finally got the idea and disappeared.

The sun was disappearing too and it was cooling down quickly. I figured no one was going to buy the Ed Hardy shirt or the $150 flannelette top, so I put them on to keep warm. The Scrabble ring had received no attention at all, so I put that on too, figuring it was a lost cause.

'Well, how'd you do?' I asked Lulu.

She'd made about twenty bucks.

'How did you go?' She asked me.

I did some maths. 'Well, if you take out rent for the stall, take out what I spent on all the jewellery and T-shirts and stuff, I think I managed to lose $70.'

'Hey, that's really good!' Lulu said.

I asked how that could possibly be good and sat down despondently to finish off my knitting while I waited for Ainsley to tell us we could go.

'Because you can't be a proper hipster if you've got money and you're good at business,' she replied. 'Hipsters don't have money.'

She had a point.

'You know what you *look* like though?' said Lulu.

I was standing there in my ultimate hipster stall wearing a tape necklace, a Scrabble ring, skinny jeans, red Ray-Bans, an ironic T-shirt and a bastardised flannelette shirt. And I was knitting a scarf.

'What?'

'You do look like the ultimate hipster. I'm not saying you *are* the ultimate hipster, but you look like the ultimate hipster.'

This made me very happy.

'Except for one little thing.'

I asked her what.

'Where's your tattoo?'

CHAPTER 8
THE ULTIMATE
HIPSTER TATTOO

Unlike shoes, haircuts and pants, tattoos cannot be changed with the season. It's therefore not surprising that up until relatively recently tattoos and fashion existed on two different and completely separate sartorial plains. Tattoos were for gangs, sailors and outlaw motorcyclists—fashion was for middle-class people with enough money or desire to change their wardrobe every year. At some point early this century the latter embraced the former and tattoos became intangibly, indelibly, irrefutably cool.

'Cool' is, of course, in the eye of the beholder. Maori warriors thought tattooing their face was cool, and it was, because they were Maori warriors and they killed people for a living. If they could scare people off before they had to do any killing it saved them time and hassle and they could get to the feasting earlier. Maori warrior tattoos on Maori warriors are, as an example, very cool. Maori warrior tattoos on people who aren't Maori warriors are not.

For a tattoo to be hipster-cool it has to meet a range of criteria—some vague, some distinct. There are a few hard-and-fast rules and the first of those is that a tattoo has to be original.

The first person to tattoo a butterfly on his or her lower back was doing something noteworthy and inspired. As were the second, third, fourth and fifth Lepidoptera fans. The one millionth person to tattoo an insect above his or her behind was merely following the crowd into the butterfly house. The same can be said for non-Asian people who got Asian symbol tattoos, people who couldn't remember what star signs they are so they had to write them permanently on their backs, and those who so feared for the safety of their upper arms that they hemmed them in with barbed wire. Trends cease to be hip once they are adopted by the mainstream. If a large portion of the tattooed population has a particular tattoo, that tattoo is not cool.

The second hard-and-fast rule is that to be hipster-cool, a tattoo must have either artistic or ironic merit. It needs to be a unique creation of beauty, or a satirical comment on something completely random. Picking a tattoo from a coffee-table book in a backstreet parlour is not cool. Getting your art-school friend to painstakingly draw you a tribute to the native fauna of an eighteenth-century English rose garden and having that emblazoned on your shoulder in a marathon six-hour session with a lesbian ink artist named Irene is cool. Drawing a moustache on the back of your index finger so that when you place your finger on your upper lip you look like Salvador Dali is also cool.

The third hard-and-fast rule is that if your right arm looks like it once belonged to Admiral Horatio Nelson, you are almost certainly on the right track. Sailors were the first Westerners to popularise tattoos and that makes their designs the most retro. Retro is cool, so anything with an anchor, a swallow or a ship is a good start. The bigger the better.

The rules regarding what not to do are equally important. Symbols of nationalism are completely out of the question—hipsters are too laid-back and left-wing for that sort of pride. Quotes are OK, in that a tattoo paraphrasing something Jack Kerouac or Oscar Wilde said is cooler than no tattoo at all, but words aren't generally seen to be trying hard enough. Tattooing your postal code onto your body is an admission that you regularly get so drunk you forget where you live. This is not to say hipsters don't regularly get so drunk they forget where they live, just that they keep their addresses stored on their iPhones rather than their shoulder blades.

I was beginning to realise, as I considered these rules, that in order to become the ultimate hipster, I was going to need a ginormous tattoo. Nothing short of mural depicting a pirate with an ironic moustache sailing on a ship made of swallows anchored to a rose garden covering my left arm was going to suffice. Virtually all my friends had agreed too—I'd taken a photo of my arm and put the call out on Facebook for recommendations on the ultimate hipster design and everyone had the same opinion—bigger was better. For someone who feared blood and needles this was daunting. Frightening, even.

I've always had issues with leaking platelets. I'd fainted half a dozen times in my life from the sight of blood, from the thought of giving blood and from having blood tests. It wasn't something I'd completely grown out of either.

The most recent fainting episode was only a few years before when I'd been on tour with a band. I'd been suffering a heinous bowel infection with a 40°C fever and there was more foul liquid coming out my back end than there was flowing out the mouth of the River Ganges. We'd made an emergency truck stop three quarters of the way between Melbourne and Sydney and after some colonic explosions that would make even the Unabomber blush I noticed that what I was wiping away wasn't light brown but dark red.

My aversion to needles meant I was never going to study medicine, but I'd learned enough about human anatomy to know shitting blood in a filthy service-station toilet on the side of the Hume Highway was as close to a medical emergency as I was going to get for a while. It didn't take long for black dots to start forming on the edges of my vision and they quickly turned into a plague of darkness. I woke up as my head hit the door in front of me and found myself eye to eye with a drawing of somebody's sizeable junk, the phone number of the apparent owner and a description of services he would gladly render if you met him in the cubicle at ten pm on any Thursday night. It nine-forty-five pm; tomorrow was Friday. I had to get out of there and fast.

Head shaken and intestines stirred, I had stumbled back to the van, explained the issue and suggested to my bandmates that someone might call a helicopter to take me to the nearest medical centre. They wanted to get some beer first and said I'd be OK, but let me have the front seat as a gesture of goodwill—it was the only one that reclined. I insisted I was dying, possibly within the hour, so our trumpet player Jake, whose uncle was a doctor in Western Australia, made a phone call to Broome and put me on speaker phone so they could record the conversation. His uncle volunteered to work in remote Aboriginal communities and had been working in rural medicine for years. Being the only doctor in an area the size of Belgium, he had attended to more broken limbs, oil rig accidents and car crash victims than I'd had hot dinners and he wasn't taking my case particularly seriously.

'What's the issue, mate?' he said.

I explained, much to everyone's mirth.

'And how long have you had diarrhoea for?'

I told him it had been for four days and that I'd had a fever initially but that had subsided.

'Have you noticed any blood in your stools until just then?'

I said no. And that I'd been checking, so definitely no.

'Well, you're not dying. If you were dying you'd be in pretty serious pain and you wouldn't be talking to me. You'd be on the ground moaning.'

I assured him I was dying.

'This blood you're talking about. Was it bright red, or just a reddish tinge?'

I told him it was bright red.

'So, as if you'd just cut yourself?'

I said yes.

'Mate, you've been wiping your arse constantly for four days, it'll be red raw and you've probably pushed a vein out a little bit from all that shitting. All you've done is just opened up a little cut on a vein on your bum. You're not dying. Take some Imodium and try not to wipe your arse as much.'

I asked him to assure me I really wasn't dying.

'You are not dying,' he said, before adding, 'you are, though, a big sooky fuck. Don't ever get a tattoo.'

The rest of the band members were by then all laughing so hard we nearly crashed. I'd always guessed I wasn't the toughest nail in the woodwork but I didn't necessarily want certified medical advice to prove it.

Getting a proper hipster tattoo was going to require some serious hardening up, though. It was also going to take a lot of commitment. I wasn't good with commitment: that was why I was on this quest in the first place. But I had no choice—a giant tattoo was the only way to ultimate hipsterdom.

But then, one Saturday morning as I was about to head out the door to meet a tattoo artist for a lengthy planning session involving an ornithology encyclopaedia, a copy of *Treasure Island* and a giant ship in a bottle, I had a call from a hipster friend I'd met at a party a few weeks before. I'd explained to her that I was on a quest to become as hip as possible and she'd been very supportive of my cause. She'd been in Berlin for a week so she'd only just seen my callout on the internet and was ringing to stop me before I made a massive mistake.

'Dude,' she said over the phone, almost panting. 'Triangle!'

'What?' I said.

'Get a triangle tattoo. That's the ultimate hipster expression. Anchors are so 2010.'

This sounded very similar to what Lulu had said when I was getting her fashion advice. I asked her what she meant.

'Google it,' she said. 'Go to Google and do a search for "triangle tattoo"—you'll see more hipsters there than if you searched for "ray-ban fixie Animal Collective crowd Brooklyn". And I just read somewhere that geometric patterns, in particular *triangles*, are about to be *everywhere* in fashion, so you're about to be *so* in. And then, of course, totally out. You'll definitely be very in for a little while though. And the good thing is, when the rest of the world is finished with the triangle fad, you can move to Tasmania and you'll be at the cutting edge again.'

I thanked her and hung up.

I opened my laptop and did the search. She was right. Triangles were starting to pop up everywhere. I sent her an e-mail by way of thanks and then noticed Hipster Radio Station Ex-Girlfriend had also e-mailed me that morning.

Hey, hope you're doing OK—I saw your tattoo callout on Facebook but didn't want to chime in or hassle you, but you should totally get a triangle tattoo. Google it. Take care and send me a picture. xx

This was too serendipitous to ignore.

I did some more searches and realised they were both onto something. Triangle tattoos were where it was at. They were so *en vogue* that a hipster band called Y△CHT had even gone to the trouble of publishing their official triangle tattoo policy as a PDF download on their website.

I quote:

Y△CHT heartily supports the wearing of all tattoos, if their value is significant to the wearer. However, for those who desire a tattoo which directly references Y△CHT, we would like to lay out some guidelines regarding that which we consider to be 'acceptable use' of the Y△CHT iconography.

Regarding the value of a Triangle tattoo, consider this. In a single figure this symbol may both reveal and conceal, for to the wise the subject of the symbol is obvious, while to the ignorant the figure remains inscrutable. The Triangle is such a rich symbolic figure that any dimension of value can be placed upon it, depending on the wearer's needs, spiritual evolution, and aesthetic concerns.

The Y△CHT Triangle tattoo is equilateral. It is not filled in. It can be inverted in any position desired and can be inked in either white or black inks. It cannot exceed, in size, a dimension of three inches. If the Triangle exceeds three inches, it cannot be called, technically, a Y△CHT tattoo. However, we do not discourage it.

The standard 'Y△CHT Triangle' tattoo is recommended for those who wish to remain oblique about the reference, those who understand the potent symbolic power of the triangle, those who are concerned with geometry, and first time tattoo-ees. If in doubt about which tattoo is right for you, consider the Triangle.

This was too good to be true. The ultimate hipster tattoo was nothing but a small, simple geometric shape which would take all of a few minutes to emblazon into my skin. There were even instructions and a style guide.

My decision was made. Now it wasn't a matter of what tattoo to get, it was a case of when.

And that time came sooner than I thought.

As it turned out, the drummer from my old band had been writing songs with a new group and their first gig had been in my calendar for a while. He lived an hour south of me on the Gold Coast and the show was slated for the upcoming Friday night. They were first on, so I'd helped them load in. A crew of friends and fans had turned up so we all went to get a bite to eat and then found ourselves standing outside a Subway restaurant with an hour to kill before they started playing. There was an airbrush tattoo stand next door and a couple of kids were throwing Skittles at seagulls and flicking through the skulls and roses trying to convince their parents to let them have some ink for the evening.

'Who wants to get a tattoo?' a friend named Jesse suddenly asked out of the blue. 'I'm going to get one, who wants to come?'

'An airbrush one?' I asked, looking over at the kids, one of whom had stopped throwing Skittles and was now throwing a tantrum.

'Huh?' said Jesse.

I pointed.

'Oh, no, ha ha, I didn't even see that. No, a real one; there're a dozen tattoo parlours around here. I created this design the other day and I want to get it done. It's only simple so it won't take long.'

I asked what it was.

'It's a triangle,' he said.

My eyes boggled.

'Are you for real?' I asked

'Yeah, it's like a triangle with two slightly elongated sides.' He drew it on his arm. 'It means you make a mistake here,' he pointed, 'you go backwards for a while, and then you wise up, change direction and come back to where you started but go on further than you did before. It's like a circle, I guess, but in triangle format.'

I'd heard all I wanted to hear.

'Follow me,' I said, dragging him by the arm before he changed his mind. 'I know a place.'

The place I knew had shut and had been replaced with a multinational, multi-storey, multi-shade-of-grey car park, but it didn't take long to find another tattoo parlour up a side street which, in the not too distant past, had been a swamp. It smelled like the cleaning closet of a hospital, which was encouraging, but the tiled walls reverberated with the buzz of two sadistic electric mosquitoes.

We asked if they could fit us in that evening. They could. 'Draw them up and come back in half an hour, we'll have everything ready,' the guy behind the counter said.

He gave us a piece of paper and a pen each. I drew a triangle. Jesse drew a triangle. We handed them back. The guy looked at them. He'd been expecting something a little more elaborate.

'OK, they'll be $110 each,' he said. 'And I'll need a $50 deposit to secure your spot.'

It seemed like a lot for a triangle, but who was I to put a price on geometry? I handed over the cash in return for a booking slip. Pythagoras would have been proud.

We returned at the appointed hour. I told Jesse I was going first. I was shaking. I didn't want to wait and watch while he got his in case I passed out.

I went in and sat down.

'Triangle?' said Brad, the tattoo artist, going over a piece of paper which had my details and a disclaimer stating that I wasn't under the influence of alcohol, under eighteen or planning to sue them if my arm fell off.

I don't know how good Brad was at tattooing people, but if a casting director was ever looking for someone to play the bouncer in a cage-fighting club frequented exclusively by pirates, he would have been a shoo-in for the part. He had more ink than I had skin.

I nodded.

'Been doing a few of those lately,' he said. 'What does it mean?'

I said it was a hipster thing. He asked me what a hipster was and put on a pair of latex gloves. I explained. He nodded.

'Like all the cool kids?' he said. I said yes.

'This your first time doing this?' he asked.

I said it was and asked him if it was his first time too. He liked my joke.

'Hold your arm out,' he said. I laid out my arm, as if about to donate blood, and he started wiping it with disinfectant solution before applying the transfer of the tattoo. It was in the right place and looked kind of cool. I held it up to show Jesse. He gave me the thumbs up.

'This is really going to hurt,' he said, dipping the needle in ink. 'You'll probably pass out from pain. Try not to let your head hit the tiles.' I looked down. 'They don't bounce as well as they look.' He was smiling. My arm was trembling.

'How long do you think it will take?' I asked.

'Mate, three minutes,' he said. 'If that.'

Three minutes was good.

'You ready?'

'Let's do this,' I said.

He hovered over my wrist with the needle. It was now or never.

'You know what other culture was into triangles?' he asked with a wry smile, raising an eyebrow.

Bang. The needle went in, I winced a little bit and the feeling was pretty much exactly as I'd guessed it would be. It bit like an iron wasp dragging its arse through my arm.

I wasn't sure where he was going with this. 'The Egyptians?' I said.

He shook his head.

'The Nazis.'

He was holding my arm now so I couldn't pull away. I nearly jumped out of the chair.

'What do you mean?' I demanded. He was already halfway along the first side. Aryan pride was so not cool.

'Yeah, a pink triangle meant you were gay,' he said. I was slightly relieved. I thought he was about to tell me Hitler had a pyramid on his ankle.

'That's not pink ink you've got there, is it?' I asked.

'Yeah.' He said deadpan, looking over beside him at the piece of paper with my signature. 'It says "pink triangle" here.'

I smiled.

'Oh well, at least if I don't have any luck tonight I can head over to a gay bar. Hello boys.'

He smiled. It was very obviously black ink, but it was a good joke.

'What did a black triangle mean?'

He worked away and thought for a bit.

'I think it meant you were an alcoholic,' he said.

That was ironic. That was good.

'No, wait, it meant you were mentally retarded.'

'What?'

'Yep.'

The other tattooist across the room laughed and looked up from his work on a girl's ankle. 'Been doing a few triangles lately,' he said. 'What band is it?'

I said there was a band called Y△CHT which had it as a symbol, but it was more of a hipster thing in general.

He looked confused. 'What's a hipster?' he asked.

Brad answered him before I could speak. 'You know, like all the cool kids,' he said, pointing at me and Jesse in turn.

The other guy nodded and went back to his ankle.

Two sides were now finished. It had taken all of two minutes. I looked back at Jesse, who was filming. I smiled and he gave me another thumbs up.

'Almost done,' Brad said. 'Doesn't hurt that much, does it?'

It didn't. It didn't tickle, though, and I was glad I wasn't getting a sleeve. Another minute of this and I was going to be happy to get out of there.

Brad buzzed away for a bit longer, carefully going over the last line.

'Done.'

And that was it.

I had a tattoo. And not just any old ink—the ultimate hipster body art. I didn't even feel slightly faint. To the contrary, I felt bold. Perhaps even a little tough.

'What are you up to now?' Brad enquired. He wrapped some tape around my wrist and told me how to take care of it.

I told him I was going to see a band.

'Oh yeah, which band?' he said.

I thought for a bit. 'You wouldn't have heard of them,' I said.

CHAPTER 9
WHAT IS HIPSTER MUSIC?

I was lying in bed. It was nine o'clock on a Saturday morning. Hipster Radio Station Ex-Girlfriend was sitting up next to me editing photos. That was how most Saturday mornings with Hipster Radio Station Ex-Girlfriend had begun. During the week she was the news-reading sidekick of the breakfast presenters — let's call them Alex and Tom. On weekends she was a professional amateur photographer. Monday to Friday she got up at quarter to four and so when Saturday came around, her version of a sleep-in was getting up at five-thirty. I usually managed to stay asleep until around nine o'clock and I would eventually be awoken by the sound of computer buttons clicking while she tried to make the light in her photos as washed out as possible before she put them on her blog.

On this particular Saturday morning the sun was streaming in through the windows, the birds were singing and everything was splendidly pleasant — apart from a screeching sound somewhere in the distance, which I assumed was an eager homeowner going about some garden maintenance. It was disturbing.

Me: Is someone sawing concrete up the road?

Hipster Radio Station Ex-Girlfriend: It's Animal Collective

playing on my MacBook; I was trying to show you some hipster music.

Me: Oh.

And thus began my formal introduction to the aural splendour of super-cool indie bands.

The problem with trying to find the ultimate hipster band is that there is no such thing as 'hipster music'. It's like hunting Keyser Söze in that movie *The Usual Suspects* — the closer you think you get, the further away you actually are and, even if you had Kevin Spacey sitting right in front of you moments ago, you would have thought he was some whining loser until one of your friends explained after he left that he was Keyser Söze all along. Tracking down the hippest band in the world is as difficult as determining the whereabouts of a mega-villain. By the time you actually find them, they're a bunch of middle-aged has-beens living in a run-down mansion in Pakistan, desperately trying to convince the world they're still relevant.

In any other musical sub-culture, finding the ultimate band would be a relatively simple task — you'd just pick the one with the highest number of record sales and the most influence on its peers. If you were choosing the ultimate punk band, for example, you could argue for a while, but you'd end up choosing either the Sex Pistols, The Clash or the Ramones.

Finding the ultimate hipster band, on the other hand, is an impossible task because the measures of success are exactly the opposite. Proper hipsters don't buy music, they download it illegally, so there are no hipster charts. Even if there were hipster charts showing what had been illegally downloaded the most, as soon as a band got to the top of the charts, all the hipsters would stop liking them because they would be seen as too mainstream.

Hipsters don't abide by any genre boundaries either, so it's not a matter of picking the most influential artist. At any given point in time the two most ultimate hipster artists will sound completely different; one will be a concrete-sawing soft-rock group from Brooklyn, the other will be a Norwegian midget who plays the banjo and makes dance music.

There are massively popular indie bands like Radiohead, The White Stripes and The Flaming Lips, which hipsters universally agree are good despite their success, but when it comes to alternative music, bigger doesn't mean more ultimate. The ultimate hipster band at any point in time will be one that very few hipsters, let alone mainstream music fans, have even heard of.

Hipster Radio Station Ex-Girlfriend had at least been some help in setting me on the path. We'd had numerous other discussions about websites to check out and bands to listen to, but she'd dumped me a week after I'd accidentally referred to one of her favourite artists as sounding like concrete being sawed, so I could no longer turn to her for advice. Even then, I don't know if it would have mattered.

I'd quizzed all her hipster radio station friends about what the ultimate hipster music was but there was no real consensus from them either, only that it was most likely made by people with beards. That didn't narrow the quest down any more, unless ZZ Top were so far ahead of the game they'd pre-empted indie rock by thirty years. I thought this was unlikely.

I'd pushed further and asked if there was some oracle of cool that all the alternative radio station programmers around the world turned to for advice, but it turned out the people in charge of choosing the nation's listening habits were being sent so much new music from record labels they didn't have time to go and find anything for themselves. The closest they got was reading magazines and going to conferences every now and then. Occasionally they'd unearth an artist from obscurity and put them on high rotation, but this was the exception to the rule. For the most part, the most played songs on alternative radio came from alternative record labels.

It made sense then to ask the alternative record labels how they determined what was cool. So I did. I called the biggest alternative record labels in the United States, the UK and Australia to find out what their secrets were and the ones who would talk to me—which weren't many— were, funnily enough, secretive.

After I begged and threatened to torture puppies until they told me, a few divulged that the process for finding a cool band was all down to their Artist and Repertoire people. I'm paraphrasing here, but in a nutshell, the A&R people's job was to smoke cigarettes, drink coffee and read blogs. If one of the blogs gave a good review to a band no one else had signed yet, they went and watched them play a show. If they could play their instruments in rhythm at least fifty per cent of the time, they offered to sign them to a record deal that paid them five cents per album for the next five albums, assigned the publishing rights of their next five hundred songs to the record label and agreed that if the band ever played a show to any more than five people, the record label was entitled to take all the money and give the band some Subway. But nothing with chicken. Chicken subs were too expensive.

'But at the end of the day, it's not just about being cool,' one indie record label executive told me. 'Being cool and making money are two very different things.'

At the end of the day, and that's when most indie record label executives got out of bed, if they thought a band was going to make them money, they just got their publicity department to tell everyone they were cool. It was as simple as that.

So there was no point then in asking record label executives who the coolest bands were. They'd just get their publicity people to tell me the bands that were cool were the ones who were going to make them the most money.

And therein lay my problem. The radio stations mostly just played the music the record labels fed them. The record labels decided what was cool based on how much money they thought they could make. None of these people were going to help me find the ultimate hipster band because the bands at the cutting edge of cool weren't making any money because as soon as they *did* start making any money they'd be accused of selling out and then they wouldn't be cool any more. It was a vicious chicken-and-egg circle, except they weren't allowed to eat the chicken.

Even if I started reading the blogs that the record company A&R people read, by the time I'd illegally downloaded the

MP3s they'd probably no longer be cool. It was beginning to look hopeless. Perhaps the ultimate hipster band was as mythical as the unicorn. What was I thinking? I could wear tight pants, get a triangle tattoo and eat only organic raspberry cupcakes, but maybe listening to the ultimate hipster music was an impossible dream. I was about ready to give up when the solution dawned on me.

The way to find the ultimate hipster band wasn't to go looking for it: it was to start it.

CHAPTER 10
THE ULTIMATE HIPSTER BAND

I was prepared for this. More prepared for this than anything I'd ever been prepared for in my life. Starting a new band had been my dream since the last one had broken up. Actually, 'broken up' was a pessimistic way of looking at it. Our singer had moved to London and our drummer and guitarist had moved to Sydney, so we hadn't technically split up, we were merely taking an artistic break to pursue other cities. Either way, I'd always been keen to create a new style of big-beat electro-dance rock music and play it in a group called The London Underground. This was my big chance.

The only problem was, The Prodigy had already created the genre in the late 1990s. They'd also had time to sell a million records and then take a ten-year break before staging a moderately successful drum 'n' bass comeback and then disappearing again. So I was a little bit late.

I also couldn't play synth. Or program a drum machine. Or sing. And the name I'd chosen for my band was the same as the public transport system in the biggest city in Europe—there might be some trademark and copyright issues. So, to be honest, starting a big-beat electro-dance rock group called The London Underground might have been a tad ambitious. It didn't really matter though, because I had three back-up band names and about twenty near-complete songs written and ready to record in a range of genres.

Or so I thought.

The back-up band names were a reality at least. I had written them down in a notebook over a period of about fifteen years. 'Henry Sugar' was the first one—named after a character in a Roald Dahl short story who could see through the back of playing cards and won lots of money at casinos. I had thought it was a great name for a band for some reason. The Black Rabbits was the second back-up name. I didn't know why I thought this was cool. I think it just sounded cute and a little bit bad. I think it used to be Black Rabbit Room, and was some sort of vague *Alice in Wonderland* reference. The last back-up band name was Suburban Empire. I'd made that up quite recently—on the way to a homemaker centre, in fact. I thought it had legs, even if it was potentially a little try-hard. It had a bit of a Rage Against the Machine vibe to it and would have been good for a hard rock band. Either way, they were all pretty solid band names, so I was already winning there.

I hadn't been quite as prolific with actual song ideas as I'd thought, though. I'd been writing songs on and off for several years and whenever something popped into my head I'd write it down. If it was a lyric it became a note on my phone. If it was a melody I'd record it into a Dictaphone app. I'd figured that I must have had a song idea every month or so since 2006, so by my calculations there should have been a cache of fifty solid-gold hits patiently waiting to be brought to life in the studio, before being taken on a stadium tour of the globe.

Much to my surprise, the total number of lyric ideas numbered eleven. One of these was already a song I'd used in my last band. Three weren't lyrics at all, but more like suggestions. For example, 'Something poetic about the landscape but not cheesy' or the not particularly helpful, 'White Stripes song but with chick from other band'. The ones which were usable were also not so much lyrics as they were a bunch of random words. 'Exotic queen chutzpah' was a case in point. That one sounded like David Bowie had been playing Scrabble and made up a song out of the last three triple-word scores. My favourite though was this:

Orchestration similar to the start of hunting for witches video features Johnny Depp who looms like nick cave painted in thick white paint like Luke steel and setting up a vintage clothing and bric-a-brac store before the start.

I'd written that one down at four in the morning after a dream I'd had in 2009. Someone must have slipped some peyote into my pear cider that night. I did think it was poignant I'd been thinking about vintage clothing market stalls for a lot longer than I'd realised, but still, it wasn't going to get me a Grammy.

The melody ideas weren't much better. There were fifteen of them all up. The best one was a complete first verse and chorus of a bluesy acoustic number. Most of them were snippets of me singing three words out of tune and then humming something inaudible for twenty seconds. None of it sounded much like a lost B-side from *OK Computer*.

Still, I'd figured I only really needed four songs and a long, cool, obscure-yet-recognisable cover to get me through. That was enough for a set. Not a headlining set, but definitely a support slot.

The real problem I was going to have was choosing a genre.

As I'd already come to realise, hipster music was impossible to pigeonhole. Punks had punk rock. Ravers had raves. Grunge had grunge. Surfers had The Beach Boys. Emos had emo, and razorblades, and hair dye. The beat generation had jazz: they stole it from the black people, but they still had it. Goths had The Cure. Tweenaged girls had Justin Bieber. Hippies had psychedelia. Dads had Neil Diamond. Mums had Norah Jones. Hipsters had everything else. There was no common thread. They liked a bit of vintage jazz, but they were more prone to Canadian art-rock, although that didn't rule out punk. 80s hip-hop was big, but not as big as chillwave or folk. The only rule of hipster music is that if you weren't the first of your friends to like a band on Facebook, they're no longer cool. Reverb also seemed to help a lot. Reverb on everything.

I didn't have any vintage jazz songs. And I wasn't from Canada. I did have reverb though. And I knew how to get some folk. So I decided to write four reverb-heavy folk songs. It was actually kind of easy.

Folk music is actually exactly the same thing as punk music. It's the same four chords, just slowed down and finger-picked on an acoustic guitar. You can take pretty much any punk song and turn it into a folk song by unplugging the guitar, singing in tune and picking out the chords instead of strumming them into a Marshall stack. At a quarter of the speed, *Anarchy in the UK* by the Sex Pistols turns into a beautiful little James Taylor protest song, best sung wearing a tie-dyed shirt on your way to San Francisco in a van. *The KKK Took My Baby Away* is a gorgeous little ditty on a nylon-string ukelele at half speed—add in some violin, a couple of hot sisters and you've basically got a Corrs concert. It's not just a punk principle either. The same theory applies to pretty much any other hit rock song ever written.

Knowing how much hipsters liked folk and reverb, I took the half a dozen decent-enough song ideas I had left, slowed them all down, added reverb and nutted out some lyrics. It only took me half an evening and it also gave me an excuse to drink whiskey on a weeknight. All proper musicians drink whiskey. It helps their voices. The more you drink and the weeker the night, the better your voice gets.

I played the songs for my flatmate Claire and she sang along with some harmonies. She asked why I was hiccupping so much. I told her I had the hiccups. She thought the songs were nice, pretty even, but that they'd be better without the hiccups. I told her she was stupid and that she didn't know anything about music. We played a game called 'Who actually has a record deal then, you or me?' and she won, but I told her that I would soon have a record deal based on the quality of my songs and the rawness of my folk reverb talent.

Claire agreed with me. She said the songs were 'lovely', and patted me on the head. I thanked her.

All I needed now was a band.

'Hey?' I said to Claire.

She said, 'What?'

'Do you want to be in my band? You can play guitar and sing.'

She said yes.

That was easy.

I wrote her name down on a piece of paper next to the words 'Backing guitar and backing vocals'. I then wrote my name next to the words 'Lead guitar and lead vocals'. Claire asked what I had written and I refused to show her, so she stole the piece of paper from me. I told her that my band needed a male singer, so it had to be me, and that I was better at guitar than her, so she had to play backing guitar. She pointed out again the fact that she had a record deal and that she should be the frontwoman but quietly accepted her fate when I threatened to lick everything in the fridge, including her shelf, and her cat, which I would put into the fridge, if she refused to give me the spotlight. I then wrote a new line for each of the other instruments I wanted, which were synth, bass, guitar and drums. I did some calculations and concluded that unless I found a particularly gifted and fashionable one-man band, a combination of talents I wasn't sure existed, I would need four more musicians. I decided the best four people to be in my band were Flea from the Red Hot Chili Peppers on bass, Jimmy Page from Led Zeppelin on guitar, Dave Grohl from Nirvana and the Foo Fighters on drums and Rick Wakeman, from, well, the 1970s on synth. I left messages on their Facebook walls and asked them to get in touch if they were free.

Presuming they might not be all free on the same date, I also made a list of friends I thought might be interested in joining the band. Jake, Sam, George and Youka were at the top of the list.

Jake had been in my last band and although he'd moved to Sydney, I knew he had been pretty keen to be involved in The London Underground. He was only twenty-one, but he was a brilliant musician and he could play any musical instrument you put in front of. When I explained the deal on Facebook and gave him a bit of background he called me straight away and said he could make it.

'You putting together a tindie band, brother?' he said.

'It's a little bit indie, I guess,' I replied. 'More hipster though. Kind of like an acoustic Animal Collective.'

'No, not indie—tindie,' he said.

'What's tindie?'

'You know. A touch of indie. Tindie.'

'I don't understand.'

He sighed. 'It's like, oh, trinket, you're trying to be a little bit indie there aren't you with your little shoes and your skinny jeans and your triangle jewellery. Tindie.'

I had no idea what he was talking about. It was like explaining why something was cool to your mum when the answer boils down to 'it just is'.

'Is tindie bad?' I asked.

He thought about this. 'It's tindie,' he said.

This didn't help me much.

'Is it good?' I asked.

There was silence on the phone.

'Well, it's a bit like hipster, I guess. If you want to be

a hipster it's good, if you don't want to be a hipster, it's bad.'

'I see.'

'Do you want to be tindie?' he asked.

I said I wasn't sure. I asked him if he was tindie. He said sometimes.

'Is tindie the same as hipster?' I asked.

He said it was similar. 'More tindie though.'

I changed the subject.

'Do you reckon your brother and George would want to be in the band?'

'Oh dude,' he said. 'They'd be mad keen.'

Sam was Jake's brother and he could sing and play the guitar. I called him and he said he was keen too. George was the drummer in a reasonably well-known metal band and he was usually off touring the country somewhere or other, but he was also uncannily free for a little while. I explained that the new band was a reverb folk group and not a metal band and he seemed to think that would be OK. He then had a long-winded one-sided conversation with me about what sort of drum kit set-up he should use for the project and whether a 21-inch or a 22-inch ride cymbal would be better. I said I didn't know. He decided 22 would be better. 'Smoother,' he said. 'Like in Bob Dylan's band The Band.' I said OK. Jake, Sam and George all sported ironic moustaches and/or hipster beard combinations so I knew they were going to be perfect.

Youka was the wildcard. I knew she was about to move to Melbourne and she was busy, so I called her up and explained that I needed a token Asian keytar player in my new hipster band and that it was very important. She agreed that every good hipster band needed a token Asian, like James Iha in the Smashing Pumpkins, and said that she would do her best but that she couldn't promise. I said that because she was Asian she was a musical child prodigy and that she didn't even need to come to any band practices — she could just turn up to gigs. She thought that sounded good but couldn't promise.

I was expecting to have to go to a back-up list of potential band members involving people with non-ironic moustaches and possibly even baggy jeans, but I'd had five wins from five hit-ups, and they were all already at least hipster*esque*, which would save a lot of time and hair straightening. Things were looking promising.

CHAPTER 11
HIPSTERECORDING

Jake, George, Sam and I were sitting in George's recording studio. Claire couldn't make it. Youka was an Asian child music prodigy so she was excused. Nevertheless, the vibe was good. Everyone was feeling pumped, except Sam, who was having a nap because he hadn't made it to bed until five am, but everyone who wasn't sleeping was in high spirits. It was the first time the band had got together and everyone was super keen to hear the amazing folk reverb hipster songs I'd written for the first time. Jake had even flown up from Sydney from it.

It had taken a while for everyone to arrive, find coffee and get settled, but a consensus had now been reached that we were about to make history. George was sitting in the engineer's seat fiddling with knobs, I was sitting cross-legged on the ground tuning a bass guitar and Jake was pacing around the place looking at pictures of all the metal bands that had recorded in the same room.

'Dude, did you know Carnal Cannibal did their first album in this very studio?' he asked, of no one in particular. I didn't know they had. I didn't even know who they were. If anything, I was worried that Jake did. He said he'd been going through a bit of a metal phase but that it was nothing to worry about.

'Sick drummer,' George piped up. 'He's using a 20-inch crash and a 17-inch double kick. So punchy.'

I didn't know what that meant either, but I was fairly certain Carnal Cannibal weren't a hipster folk band.

'So what sort of vibe are we going for?' asked George, playing with a red thing on a mixing desk—I don't know the technical name for it. I think it made the reverb louder, which was good.

I explained that it was sort of a folky reverb thing and very hip. Sort of like Fleet Foxes. Fleet Foxes were a harmony-laden hipster folk band that had just received an 8.8 out of 10 review on Pitchfork.com. This meant they were hipster-good, although not as good as they were when they released their first album, which got a 9 out of 10.

'Cool,' said George. 'So lots of harmonies.'

I hadn't thought about this.

'Yes,' I said. 'Lots of harmonies.'

Everyone nodded. Even Sam, who had just woken up and was rubbing his eyes. This renewed my confidence in their ability to not play metal.

'OK, and, like, acoustic guitar, bass, drums, electric guitar, yeah?' George was pulling out microphone leads and cables and things so we could set up. I nodded.

He plugged some things in and did some checks of levels. We all played around for a little bit. This took half an hour. Eventually all the little lights lit up on the screen in the appropriate places to indicate sound was coming out of our instruments at the right levels.

'OK, play us the first song,' George invited.

I strummed and sang. Everyone thought it was nice. Sam thought it was cool. 'Very folky.' This was promising.

I showed everyone their parts. It was only four chords stretched into a verse part and a chorus part, so it didn't take long until everyone assured me they had it. I thought things sounded good, but a little dry, so I asked George to turn up the reverb on my guitar as far as it went. He did. I asked him to do the same for my vocals. It sounded like I was playing a guitar in a shower in a cave in a cathedral—a cathedral that used to be a reverb-effects-unit manufacturing plant before they made it a cathedral. It wasn't quite enough reverb for my liking but George said that was as much as he could add without the echoes drowning out the actual song.

There was some adjusting of headphones and after another fifteen minutes of going to the toilet, finding beer, drinking beer and talking to various girlfriends and mothers on the phone it looked like we might be ready to start.

'OK,' I said, looking around the room. 'Everyone ready?' They all nodded. 'Roll the tape.' It wasn't actually tape, it was just a computer with Pro Tools, but 'roll the tape' sounded cooler. We started playing.

It's hard to describe music with words. That's why it's music. You need to be able to hear to describe music in much the same way as you need to have seen the colour blue to know what it is. If you were forced to illustrate 'blue' to someone who couldn't see, you might say it looked something like how having the first snow of the season fluttering gently onto your outstretched palm might feel—or perhaps the sensation you get when you dive into the ocean at the very start of summer when it's not quite warm enough yet but you've spent an hour getting to the beach and you'll be buggered if you're not taking a dip anyway. That feeling.

It would be impossible to use words to give an accurate representation of the first recorded moments of the world's newest, most ultimate hipster band, but if you had to give it a crack, 'concrete', 'falling', 'on raccoons', 'mating', and 'inside a garbage bin factory staffed by schizophrenic monkeys' would probably be among them.

The track finished.

'What did you think?' Jake asked me. For some reason he'd ambitiously decided to switch from playing guitar to playing bongos halfway through the track. 'I added some colour there in the middle.' It would have been overpowering had George not decided to join him with an extended and unannounced drum solo after the second chorus.

I nodded. It was a colour all right.

They were all looking at me expectantly. Like when a puppy brings home a decomposing rat carcass and puts it on your pillow to wake you up in the morning.

'It was definitely loud enough,' I said. 'The fuzz pedal on the bass made it interesting too, Sam. You're definitely not asleep any more are you, buddy?'

They were beaming.

We had the studio booked for eight hours and the first run-through of the first song had taken us nearly three. We'd also all turned up an hour and a half late, which meant we were halfway through the session and we had four minutes of recording done. Unless Bob Dylan walked into the room with Thom Yorke, I had a feeling we weren't going to get a lot of hipster folk recorded. I needed a plan. And fast. I didn't have Bob Dylan's phone number either, so that wasn't an option.

I thought for a while. They looked at me thinking. Lucky I had my glasses on—I looked smart, so they paid attention quietly. There was clearly no way we were going to be able to learn, record and mix four intricate little four-minute folk numbers in four hours. But what if I put the folk-is-sloweddown-punk theory in reverse? And what if instead of being punk, which was a little passé, we put our flannelette to use in the Kurt Cobain-like manner that God intended?

'OK,' I said. 'Here's the plan. We're not a hipster reverb folk band any more. We're now a grunge band. A Korean hipster grunge band.'

This confused them. This confused them a lot.

George was the self-appointed back-up leader of the group and it was up to him to gingerly point out the fact that no one was Korean and that grunge wasn't cool.

'I know,' I said. 'That's the point.'

They were still looking in need of an explanation.

'What are we all wearing?' I asked. 'Apart from instruments.'

They looked at their shirts. We all had flannelette on.

'And who wears flannelette?' I prodded.

'Lumberjacks,' said George. I said he was close.

They all thought about this for a while, and then it dawned on them. Grunge bands wore flannelette.

'Do you know any other grunge bands at the moment? New ones?' I asked. No one did.

'Well, it can only be a matter of days before some other hipster takes a look at the fucking shirt they're wearing and has the same idea. And until then, we're the first. Which makes us the ultimate hipster band.'

'And even if someone else has had the same idea before us, we'll still be the only *Korean* grunge band.'

George pointed out the fact that since he'd last checked, which was only moments before, no one had become Korean.

'Youka is half Japanese,' I told him. 'That's close enough.'

'But what about your four folk songs?' Jake asked.

'We're just going to play them at twice the speed, twice the volume, and with twice the number of amplifiers. We'll still have four songs, but instead of them being intricate four-minute folk reverb songs, which will take forever to record, they'll be simple two-minute punk songs. We can knock them over in four hours, easy.'

Everyone had to admit I had a point.

And lo and behold, it worked. We got them all recorded in time. Sam even had time for another nap in between takes of 'Hari Kari is Cool' and 'Kim Jong Il Ate My Baby' (I had to change the titles around from the original folk versions a little, but the melodies stayed the same).

We played the recordings back. They actually sounded pretty good.

It came time to bounce down the tracks so we could all take them home and have a listen. George was putting them onto a CD when he realised he needed to call them something. I gave him the names of the songs.

'And what's the name of the band?' he asked.

I hadn't thought of this. It had to be the ultimate hipster band name. The Black Rabbits wasn't going to cut it. Nor was Suburban Empire. I already knew The London Underground was out. I asked the guys if they had any ideas. They had a think.

George said it should be something ironic. We all agreed. 'The Black Fly Chardonnays,' Sam suggested. 'Like the Alanis Morissette song'. I told him he was ghey and that the world's greatest hipster band ever wasn't going to be named after an Alanis Morissette song. He argued it was ironic. I said Alanis Morissette wasn't yet ironic, just ghey. He said I was wearing an Ed Hardy T-shirt. We called it a draw.

Everyone went back to thinking. My tattoo was still healing and I was absent-mindedly rubbing it while we thought. Jake was looking at me, concentrating.

'Dude, I've got it!' he suddenly said, almost jumping out of his seat as he pointed to my wrist. 'The Triangles!'

I thought this was pretty cool. It was certainly hipster. I Googled it on my phone. Sadly, there was already a band called The Triangles. It was an Australian band that had apparently had a hit single in Spain after one of their songs appeared on a Spanish beer commercial. The YouTube clip had even had 3.2 million views. It was kind of good actually.

'What about Triangular?' I asked. They thought this had merit. 'But that'll be too hard to find on the Internet. All the domain names and social media usernames will be taken.' They also agreed.

'Triangulr, then,' I said. 'With no "a" at the end, like tumblr, and flickr, but Triangulr.'

George wrote it down to see how it looked. It looked OK but not perfect. It was a bit too long and jumbled.

I had an idea and asked George for the pen. 'Hold your breath,' I said.

I knocked out the 'U' and the other 'A' and wrote:

TRI△NGLR

There was a moment of silence.

It was perfect.

We all stood back to admire it.

'You know where that would look great?' Jake said.

'Where?' I asked.

'On a gig poster.'

I hadn't thought about that.

'You have organised a gig, haven't you?'

'Yeah, no, of course,' I said. I was lying through my teeth. I had done nothing of the sort.

'Cool,' said George. 'Where is it?' He'd called my bluff.

I named the tindiest bar in Brisbane.

'Oh yeah,' said Jake. 'That's perfect. Nice. I didn't think they had bands.'

'They don't usually,' I said. 'But I made friends with the owner the other day and they said they'd be happy to make an exception for us. It's on my birthday actually, so I kind of said we'd book the place out for a private party. They were cool with that.'

I was making it up, but I figured they'd be keen to have us—even if it was super-early or super-late. We made arrangements to have another practice at Sam's house the day of the show, just to make sure we were ready.

We were about to leave when Sam piped up.

'Hey, umm, there's one other thing still missing then,' he said, looking coy.

'What?' I asked. 'That name is perfect. We have our first gig.'

'I know,' he said. 'But if we want to be the ultimate hipster band, we need to do more than just call ourselves TRI△NGLR. Let's put an ad in the street press and find ourselves a TRI△NGL player. And instead of saying "must have own transport", like all the other musician-wanted ads do, ours can say "must have own fixed-gear bicycle".'

It was probably the most genius idea anyone had ever had.

'Which reminds me, Matt,' he continued. 'I can't help but notice you turned up to band practice in a motor vehicle. If you're supposed to be the ultimate hipster, where the fuck is your fixie?'

The man did indeed have a point.

CHAPTER 12
TRIXIE THE FIXIE

I can totally understand why hipsters have a fixie fixation. They are the preferred mode of transport for the coolest of the cool because fixed-gear bicycles are the most endearing form of transport on the planet. They don't pollute anything for a start, which means every kilometre you ride offsets the five gabillion tonnes of atmospheric carbon that goes into making a 12-inch vinyl Radiohead LP. They look absolutely splendidly, properly retro too, like the bike your grandfather might have had sometime after the war, so they are unarguably cool.

They're also incredibly pretty. More specifically, you can get any part of the bicycle in any colour of the rainbow, which makes them infinitely customisable and immeasurably unique. If you want a purple seat, pink tyres, a white chain and orange rims, you can knock yourself out—and the stranger the combination, the better. If the colour scheme of your bike doesn't look like it was inspired by a chainsaw massacre inside a Skittles factory, you're not trying hard enough. As a result, unlike mass-produced mainstream mountain bikes, no two fixies look the same. They are a statement of individuality.

Keeping with the quirks, fixies only have one gear and

literally four moving parts (including the wheels) so even the most mechanically-retarded city-dwelling machineophobe can easily pull bits off and replace them without breaking a nail or a sweat. They are low maintenance and low cost without being low-brow, and they snub their noses at conventional authority with no reflectors, no logos, no mudguards, no bells and no lights.

Despite their simple and obvious charms though, fixies are far from faultless. In fact, fixed-gear bicycles in their purest form suffer two flaws so terrible they are quite literally fatal. Flaw number one is that proper fixies have no brakes.

Deceleration devices are a luxury which can be done without if you live in the Maldives. In any other part of the world brakes are generally regarded as non-optional. Brakeless bicycles are bombshells. They are a date with Pamela Anderson—pretty to look at, if you like that sort of thing; you know you're in for a good time, but at the end of the day (or in the middle of the day on your boat) your partner has hepatitis C and you're going to get messed up. The only way you can stop on a proper fixie is by bunny-hopping the rear wheel up and using the sheer force of your leg muscles to lock the wheel mid-air before dropping it down into a skid. It's not easy at ten kilometres per hour on a flat bicycle path. On a steep hill you'd be quite literally safer BASE jumping.

The 'fixed' in fixed-gear bicycle also means quite literally that. It doesn't mean your choice of gears is fixed at one, it means the gear is literally stuck in place, so when you stop pedalling, the pedals keep moving. The result is that you can't just stand up and coast like you would on any other bike, you HAVE to keep pedalling all the time whether you want to or not. It doesn't sound like a big deal, and most of the time it isn't, until you come across a hill. Or a corner. Gears were invented so bikes could go up inclines easily. On a fixie, you need quadriceps of carbon fibre to go up, and the legs of Speedy Gonzales to go down. It's comical to behold, and tiring to try. If you go around a corner too quickly you're also highly likely to hit the pedal on the ground on the way around, which will throw you off the bike and into the path of oncoming traffic. (Slowing yourself down to go around a corner isn't all that easy when you don't have any brakes either.)

Most average hipsters avoid these two problems by simply fitting a non-fixed gear to the rear wheel and brakes to the front. It doesn't make going uphill any less taxing, but it does mean you can cruise downhill without killing yourself. On the whole, it makes riding a lot easier and hipsters, as we know, are an effort-shy bunch.

I was by now, though, not your average hipster. I'd made craft, I'd tattooed a triangle to my skin and started the ultimate hipster band. Short of getting a gig on a side stage at Coachella, getting a fixie was probably the single biggest hipster statement I was going to be able to make, and I was going to do it properly. No brakes. No gears.

All I had to do now was figure out how to build a bicycle.

You can buy a fixie off the shelf in the right kind of bike shop, of course, but it completely defeats the purpose. The whole point of being a hipster is making retro stuff yourself. Having someone else build your bicycle at a factory in Phnom Penh is like marrying Angelina Jolie/ Brad Pitt and getting another person to make your babies. You can do it, but the tabloids will seriously question your sanity and you'll just end up taking advantage of a small, impoverished Asian nation.

The only proper way to become a fixie rider is to buy the parts on the internet and build the bike yourself from scratch. In an ideal world you'd lurk on eBay for six years until the widow of an Italian velodrome champion, who was involved in a tragic accident during the 1956 tour of Florence which killed him but miraculously didn't scratch the bike, decided to auction off all his old equipment. Ideally you'd get the parts, which had presumably been kept under the house in vacuum-sealed storage bags since the Melbourne Olympics, for a sum not greater than $40 and use the frame as the basis for your fixie. You'd then frequent bike shops around your city, chat to their owners about tattoos and purchase a titanium bolt each week for a period of nine months, or until you had enough bolts to build a bike—whichever took the longest—and then, on a series of non-concurrent weekends, you would put the thing together, sand-blast everything to strip back the paint, feed a small child a packet of crayons and punch it in the tummy until it vomited in the general direction of your project, let it dry and then upload a photograph to your tumblr account before declaring your creation 'finished'.

In an ideal world, that would be the ultimate hipster fixed-gear bicycle. I liked the idea, but I wasn't living in an ideal world. I was working to a schedule and I didn't have time to wait for an Italian frame to appear out of the ether. I didn't have a toolkit either, or any patience. So I cheated.

Jellybean Bikes was the name of the company. They had a cool website where you could build a virtual fixie by choosing all the colours of the components. They showed you a picture of what it looked like and you then handed over your credit card details so they could build it for you in a warehouse in Victoria and ship it off, ninety per cent assembled, in three to four working days. The ninety per cent assembled bit was key. Ninety per cent assembled meant that it was ten per cent *un*assembled. Which meant that, technically, I would be responsible for building the thing myself. Technically I was buying the 'parts' on the internet and building a bike with my heart and soul. No one had to know that I was only responsible for putting on the seat and tightening the pedals, and that my toolkit consisted of a spanner I'd found at bottom of my sock drawer and a couple of Allen keys I'd had lying around since I bought that bookshelf at IKEA.

The five hundred bucks they were asking was also going to work out a lot cheaper than buying a titanium bolt each week for nine months, so I placed my order.

The next day I got a call from Sam at Jellybean Bikes.

Sam: Hey, is that Matt?

Me: Yes it is.

Sam: Oh hey, Matt, it's Sam here from Jellybean Bikes.

We've got your order here, it's all good, but I just wanted to check, you've ticked the box which says you want the gear fixed?

Me: Yep.

Sam: OK, cool. Cool. You know that means you can't coast, right, and that the pedals will keep moving all the time.

Me: Yep, I know. Is that OK?

Sam: Yeah, yeah, of course, it's just that, well, not many people tick that box and we usually give them a call just to check that's what they want. Someone had a bit of an, well, an accident, and we just like to check.

Me: Nah, all good, Sam. Fix me up.

Sam: OK, so you know you can flip the rear wheel around and use the cog on the other side if you like, that one isn't fixed. Then you can coast if you want.

Me: Yep, I saw that.

Sam: OK, cool. Just checking. All right then. I'm going to make your bike now.

Me: OK. Hey, when you say 'going to make my bike now', it doesn't come, like *totally* assembled, does it? There's still a bit of spanner work for me to do, isn't there?

Sam: Oh nah mate, you just need to put the seat on and screw in the pedals and you'll be right. We do most of it. The new box is pretty cool. Ships in one package.

Me: But, I need like, a spanner to screw in the pedals, don't I?

Sam: Well, yeah, they need to be on pretty tight.

Me: So technically, like, *I'm* the one finishing off the

bike-building process, aren't I? I mean, you couldn't ride it without pedals and a seat could you?

Sam: Well, I guess, if you put it that way, I suppose. No.

Me: OK cool.

Sam: Cool.

Me: OK, so when do you think I'll have the bike?

Sam: Well, I'll try and get it with the courier tonight, so you should have it tomorrow or the next day.

This was good news. True to his word, Sam did get my ninety-per-cent finished bike on the courier run that evening; and three days after I ordered it, a brown carton arrived on my doorstep. I tore open the box, whipped out my tools and after a good ten minutes of soulful spanner work, I had a fixie, and she was gorgeous. Everything on her was matt black, apart from the tyres, which were red, the rims, which were spearmint, and the chain and hubs, which were bright orange.

All she needed was a name.

I considered 'Minty' because of the rims, but that sounded too much like a lolly. She was all black, so I was going to go with an African American name, like Beyonce, or Nina Simone, but that was a tad formal for a bicycle. It had to be something cute. Preferably something that rhymed with 'fixie'. Ditsy was out. Bitsy sounded like a dog you'd pick up, or drop off, at an animal shelter. Mitsy was too similar to a character from a picture book for three-year-olds.

'Trixie', on the other hand, was perfect.

A year ago I'd met a guy called Josh and a bunch of his friends who'd curated the Sydney Bicycle Film Festival. I'd first been introduced to them by Dave at an arts festival in Newtown, where they'd set up a stall with all kinds of fixed-gear bicycle paraphernalia and I'd jovially ribbed them for not having brakes on their preferred mode of transport. When we got talking and they told me that not only were there enough people sufficiently into fixies to make films about them, but that there were enough films about them to warrant an entire festival, I stopped being amused and started being impressed. I usually associated niche film festivals with transgender *Star Trek* fans, but this sounded hardcore and cool.

I never actually made it to the festival—in fact I'd ended up drinking one too many ciders that day and completely forgotten about it—but now that I had a fixie I decided to get online and find some of the videos they were talking about as inspiration. Sure enough, there were hundreds. Most of them involved people skidding gracefully down hills in San Francisco. Towards the end of each film there would be a mashup of all the bloopers, which usually involved hipsters smashing into cars. It wasn't pretty. I mean, it was pretty filmmaking, but it was pretty ugly for the people on the bikes. There were also lots of references to bike polo. Bike polo appeared to take place on a flat surface. Smashing mallets into polo balls on disused basketball courts looked a lot safer than smashing hipsters into cars on asphalt mountains.

Brisbane is a hilly city. Not quite as hilly as San Francisco, but compared to New York, London, Sydney or Melbourne,

Brisbane is positively Himalayan. As a result, it wasn't the ideal habitat for a first-timer on a fixed-gear bicycle. My street was flat, so the maiden voyage from my front door to the other side of the road and back was wobbly, but reasonably uneventful. If I was going to be the ultimate hipster fixie rider, though, I'd need to venture further than my neighbour's house. Bike polo seemed like the perfect way to get a feel for Trixie without losing a limb. A quick Google search revealed there was even a Brisbane Bike Polo Club, which met in a park across town every Sunday at two pm. That was the next day.

The park was one of those seedy ones in which people used syringes more than swings—not the kind of place you'd go for a picnic, but I figured there had to be safety in numbers. Besides, the kind of people who rode bikes with no brakes for fun would surely be tougher than any junkie. The website seemed friendly too: all I had to do was just show up—no experience necessary.

I arrived at the park at two pm on the dot. It had been a relatively incident-free journey for my first big ride. The only scare I had was towards the end when a vicious-looking Rottweiler came hurtling out of a yard towards me like a slingshot, snarling its head off and foaming at the mouth as if it had rabies. The gate was open and I thought I was done for, but unbeknownst to me the dog was chained up to a wire runner which was hidden in the long grass, and as it got to the footpath its neck snapped back and arced in the opposite direction like it was on a bungee cord. That had thrown me a little, but at least I'd arrived ungrazed.

I scoped out the surroundings and started thinking about how to introduce myself to what would undoubtedly be a lively bunch of hipsters just about to start their match. 'No, you guys start without me: I'm still getting used to this thing so I'll just watch for a bit,' I was thinking I'd say. Then they'd insist I join in immediately and put me under the wing of an experienced captain who would praise my choice in wheel colours and comment on how quick I was at picking the game up. He'd ask if I was sure I'd never played bike polo before and tell me I was a natural before I'd shrug a little and admit that I used to mountain bike a bit as a teenager and that I guessed I probably had a bit of a knack for it.

But there was no one around and there was a slight drizzle falling from the sky. I didn't know a lot about bike polo conditions, but instinct told me wet concrete wasn't ideal. At least no one was shooting up heroin under a tree, which gave the place a slightly more pleasant ambience than I'd otherwise expected. There were a couple of dodgy-looking guys sitting down on an old basketball court drinking beers, but that was it for company. They had bicycles with them but the chains were black and they were wearing heavy metal band T-shirts, so I figured they couldn't possibly be polo players. There weren't any sticks or balls in sight and they certainly didn't look like they were gearing up for a bit of sport.

I skirted the park once more and couldn't see any obvious hordes of hipsters so I just presumed the website was out of date and decided to head home again. Despite the light rain it had been a nice ride over to this part of town, so I wasn't exactly disappointed—I could get an ice cream on the way home too. It had been a while since the blog had been updated anyway and there were no contact numbers or anything listed so I wasn't surprised. At least I'd tried.

The two dodgy-looking lads were sitting in pretty much exactly the spot the website had described though, so I decided to ride past again a little closer and just see if I could get their attention. I was a little nervous. This wasn't the wisest part of town for a lone, skinny hipster to be enquiring about polo matches. It was a bit like rocking up in Brixton or Harlem or Frankston in a convertible SAAB and asking a bunch of crack dealers directions to the country club. At best I'd get spat on; at worst, stabbed. Still, I'd come all this way, so it would be a shame to leave now if there was a game about to start, even if it was between me and the two original members of Metallica.

Original member of Metallica one: Hey man, what's happening?

Me: Hey, umm, is this the, ah, bike polo place?

Original member of Metallica two: Sure is, bit quiet today though.

Me: Cool, I'll pedal around.

I rode around the edge of the tennis court and up a hill. They were watching me closely. I was trying not to fall off and hoping it wasn't some sort of hipster trap. What if an anti-hipster gang had set up a fake website to lure in impressionable young cool kids to the dodgiest park in the city before beating them to death with polo mallets and stealing their gold bicycle chains?

Me: Hi.

Original member of Metallica one: Hey, man. Nice to see you. Are you from around here?

Me: No, I live in New Farm.

He nodded.

Original member of Metallica one: You picked a slow day, I'm afraid.

He took a sip of what I had thought was a beer, but which, upon closer inspection, proved to be pear cider. I let out an audible sigh of relief.

Original member of Metallica one: Yeah, the nationals are on today in Adelaide so everyone's either there or on the Gold Coast for a tournament. It's just me and Red up here today, I think. I'm Andy, by the way.

He stuck out his hand. I shook it.

Me: I'm Matt; nice to meet you.

I leaned my bike up against the chain-link fence and sat down on the asphalt. Andy and Red weren't criminals. They were fixie fans. And they were the real deal. Red was covered in scars and had on some sort of padded gloves. Their bikes had no brakes and no reflectors, just a set of handlebars and fancy branding on every component. The pedals had straps on them and the chains looked like they were made from leftover metal from a rocket ship. They looked at my bike and then back at me, and then back to my bike. I felt like I'd walked into an ultimate fighting octagon wearing a primary-school tae kwon do uniform.

Red looked confused.

Red: What sort of frame is that? Is it new?

Me: Umm, it's black.

Red nodded slowly. The way a crocodile would nod if you asked if the water was warm.

Andy asked me a question about building it myself. He used lots of words I didn't understand, but from what I could tell he was asking me if I'd used spanners and other similar tools to change the bike from being a pile of parts into something you could pedal.

Me: Sort of. I bought it online. It came in a box yesterday so I had to put the pedals and seat on. There's a company in Melbourne that makes them. I think they buy all the parts in China or something and then you choose the colours and they make your bike. It was only five hundred bucks.

Andy nodded politely. Red said reassuringly that it was 'a lot of bike for the money' but we all kind of knew it was as if I'd turned up at a big wave surfing contest in Hawaii on a fifty-foot day wearing Speedos and diving flippers and announced I was going to compete on my bodyboard. Still, they were giving me points for being interested.

Me: So how many people usually turn up?

Red: Usually maybe twenty or so. We have a bit of fun. Everyone has a few ciders and then we play until sunset. It's pretty casual but we had the nationals here last year and it can get reasonably serious.

I was aware of only four other sports in which the consumption of alcohol was stipulated by law for all participants: golf, darts, pool and lawn bowls. Golf was, as Mark Twain put it, the best way to ruin a good walk. Lawn bowls required more patience than I had and I couldn't in all honesty define as a sport an activity which required less arm effort than masturbation, so pool and darts certainly didn't count. Mixing cider and fast bicycles with no brakes, on the other hand, sounded like an ideal way to spend a Sunday afternoon.

Andy: But I don't know if anyone else is going to show today. Dave has the mallets and the key to the witches' hats.

He motioned to some orange cones that were chained to the fence.

Me: Hmm, might not be the best day for a game then.

Andy: Nah, but you should come back next weekend. What are you doing next weekend? It's the Bike Courier Nationals.

There seemed to be more national championships in this sport than there were weekends in a year.

Me: Oh actually. I was supposed to be auditioning triangle players for a band.

Red: What?

Me: That can wait. I'm free. I'll come along.

Red: Man, it'll be crazy. One big party. All the bike couriers will be up from Sydney and everyone just drinks for the whole weekend. Get here at midday and you'll have a hell of a time.

CHAPTER 13
THE NATIONAL BIKE COURIER BIKE POLO CHAMPIONSHIPS

It was bike polo day. Not just any bike polo day, but National Bike Courier Bike Polo Championships Day. This was like the Superbowl. And the Olympics, rolled into one. Only with hipsters. And cider. I was excited.

I'd been looking up bike polo YouTube videos all week, writing down little tips and then practising. From what I could tell, all the best players blocked up their wheels with some sort of covering to prevent mallets and balls crashing through, so I'd made some nicely fitted covers out of old pizza boxes. I figured they'd hold up well as long as it didn't rain.

I'd been practising tricks out the front of my house too. Bunny-hopping was the most crucial move to learn — jumping up a gutter was how you got out of the way of oncoming buses when you were heading downhill in traffic. I was getting quite good at it as well. In fact, I was at the stage where if a Matchbox car happened to career out of the hands of a small child and into my path, I stood a real chance of being able to clear it outright.

Riding with no hands was another important skill. Mastering that was absolutely essential in order to be able to hold a mallet and raise a cider to your lips at the same time. I didn't have a mallet to practise with, so I'd been honing my skills with a broom and a plastic water bottle. I'd even borrowed some witches' hats from the roadworks at the end of the street to practise weaving around. My record was three weaves and a U-turn before I had to put my foot down. I didn't know who was on the world National Bike Courier Bike Polo Championship team, but I was fairly certain of a call-up once they saw me in action.

Riding half-drunk was the other core competency I'd been working on. I'd already had a bit of experience with this one, although none of it professional. I knew I could get a normal bicycle home from my mate Ian's place with a kebab in hand at three am on a Saturday, so riding around semi-drunk on a fixie in the daylight was probably an equal grade of difficulty. I'd done a few dusk test runs after some vino and, as long as I went slowly, I seemed to be quite OK at it.

I had nothing to worry about on National Bike Courier Bike Polo Championships Day though. The sun was bright, the conditions were fair and my spirits were high as I set off from my house at eleven am. I'd allowed an hour to get across town so I could take the scenic route by the river. It was a bit longer than cutting across the CBD, and it still involved going past the Rottweiler, but the dog could only get as far as the footpath anyway, so I was in no danger.

I felt like the king of the world as I pedalled along on Trixie. She was matt black, so there was no cheeky glinting in the sun, but every other cyclist I passed looked at me longingly and there were nods from everyone. It didn't matter whether they were hardcore road cyclists wearing painted-on Lycra or small children out on their training wheels with Mum and Dad, everyone looked longingly at Trixie and gave me a little smile as if to say 'what a splendid bicycle you have there'.

One boy, he must have been about nine, saw me riding along and I heard him ask his parents why I didn't have a helmet on.

'Well, obviously he's too *cool* to wear a helmet, he doesn't *care* if he smashes his head open on the concrete,' the dad said. He was being sarcastic but the kid wasn't having a bar of it.

'I want to be cool too!' he replied. 'Dad, I want to be cool! Did you see his bike? He had red wheels! Can I get red wheels?'

The dad scowled at me as he passed but I just gave him the broadest smile I could and wished him a lovely day. His son was right. I was cool.

There was a bottle shop about three quarters of the way there and I didn't want to arrive at the match empty-handed so I stopped in to grab a six-pack of cider. I hadn't thought to purchase a bike lock and I was wary of leaving Trixie out the front in that part of town unchained, so I walked her into the store and leaned her up against the ice machine while I went to get the drinks. I could see the checkout guy staring at her enviously.

'Nice bike,' he said when I came to the counter.

'Thanks,' I replied.

'New, is it?' he asked.

'Yep. Got it the other week.'

He nodded. 'Looks fancy: what'd that set you back?'

I eyed him suspiciously. He had a goatee, and proper tattoos, and looked like the kind of guy who had mates who owned baseball bats but didn't play baseball. I wondered if he was about to make a call to inform them a hipster with a real fancy set of wheels had arrived, fresh from the city. He'd probably spit tobacco on the ground while he spoke.

'Oh, I built it myself actually,' I said. 'The parts are pretty cheap, so it's not worth much, hey. Just sentimental value really.'

'Oh right.'

There was an awkward silence while I waited for him to scan the cider. He was looking the handlebars up and down.

'You got backpedal brakes on that thing?' He finally asked.

'Oh, well, sort of. Not really: there aren't any brakes, so you have to literally pedal backwards to stop.'

'You're kidding me.' He sounded impressed now.

'Nope. You lean forwards, flick the back wheel up, lock it with the pedals and then let it fall back down again so it skids out sideways. It's pretty easy once you get the hang of it.'

'Well I'll be . . .' he said, and scanned the cider. 'That's pretty hardcore, man. Respect. These are on special too.' He winked and put the six-pack into a plastic bag. 'Staff discount.'

'Thanks.' I said. Maybe this part of town wasn't as rough as I'd thought.

I left the store and wrapped the plastic bag around the handlebars tightly so the cider hung down below and didn't wobble around too much. I didn't have far to go now but I didn't want to risk smashage this early in the game. It was a reasonably snug fit, but one of the bottles was rubbing up too closely to the wheel. It would be better if they sold cider in five-packs, I thought.

I started riding off, but the bottle on the corner was making such a nuisance of itself I ended up snapping it away from the six-pack and holding it in my hand. That was much better.

Other than a brief stop at the bottle shop, I had been riding for almost an hour by then and had built up a bit of a thirst, so I figured rather than let the drink go warm in my palm I might as well crack it open and treat myself. It was practically midday anyway, and I was willing to bet midday was cider-o'clock in bike-polo circles. I took a swig. It was the ultimate hipster thing to do really.

All my practice with the water bottle earlier in the week was now paying off and, as long as I didn't ride too fast, I was able to pedal along with the cider in one hand and the handlebars in the other. I even did a few quick pretend polo moves with my non-cider hand and imagined the ball sailing through the goals and the crowd cheering.

The imaginary crowd was going nuts and I was up to my fifth goal by the time I rounded the corner and came past the rabid Rottweiler's house. I was on the other side of the street, but just like last time, he saw me coming and came bolting towards Trixie at a million miles an hour.

The gate was open again and he had a clear view of me so I rode no-hands and gave him a cheeky little middle finger salute as I passed. I even slowed down a little so I could watch him rebound off the end of the tether. He got to the footpath even quicker than last time and I waited for the bungee motion. But it didn't come. He didn't stop running. In fact, he wasn't tied up at all. And he was heading straight for me. Rather quickly. And foamily.

I'm not usually a big user of swear words but the expletives that left my mouth could have made a pirate blush. I don't know that yelling every curse I knew had any effect in scaring the dog: in fact, if anything it seemed to get him more excited, but it sure as hell fired me up. Without any gears to change through I hit top speed in about five seconds flat and had managed to make some decent ground on the Rottweiler before I noticed I was heading for a stop sign and there was a car coming towards me from my right-hand side.

I had no time to swerve out of the way so I instinctively reached out with the fingers on my right hand to slam on the brakes. By the time I realised there weren't any I was a couple of metres away from the bonnet of the white utility. The driver saw me and managed to get a bit of emergency braking done, but it was too late, we were heading straight for the car. I tried my best to pull off a bunny hop, but I only got a few millimetres off the ground and Trixie and I hit the front quarter panel with an almighty crash.

The impact sent me slightly airborne and I landed with a thud by the wheel just as the Rottweiler closed in. I tried to get up and run away, but Trixie was on top of me and there was a stabbing pain in my ankle as soon as I put weight on it, so the best I could do was throw my arms over my head and start praying.

I winced and waited for the rabid jaws to close around my throat but, strangely, nothing happened. I kept my eyes closed for a bit longer but the only thing I could feel was something furry swooshing in my face.

I opened one eye, and then the other. The Rottweiler was wagging its tail and munching something. It had its arse in my nose so I couldn't see what. I figured I was probably paralysed from the waist down and it was now devouring my broken leg so I craned my neck a little harder to see, and then realised it was licking one of the pizza boxes I'd woven into the front wheel.

I smiled briefly and let out an enormous sigh of relief, but my joy was short-lived as I looked at the bonnet of the vehicle. There were some little specks of Trixie paintwork scraped on it. I was concerned, but then I realised the specks of paint hadn't scratched the car itself, just one of the stickers on it—one of the blue-and-white chequered stickers.

'Are you all right, mate?' the constable asked me, getting out of the car. His partner came and joined him on my side.

'Going a bit fast there.' He looked me up and down.

I pointed to my ankle and groaned.

'Can you move it?' the partner asked.

I tried to move it.

'Yeah, a little bit,' I said. 'It fuc— It really hurts though.'

'If you can move it, it's probably not broken,' he said. 'See if you can get up.'

I stood up. I was still holding a cider in one hand. I'd

tried not to let it go so it wouldn't smash. The rest of the six-pack was cactus though. There was booze everywhere.

'What have you got there?' the first officer asked me, nodding his head at the drink in my hand.

'Pear cider,' I said. Looking sheepish.

'Pear cider,' he said.

'Where are you off to?' he asked.

'Bike polo,' I said.

'Bike polo,' he said. I wondered if he was going to repeat everything I said.

'You just went through a stop sign there, mate. A bicycle is considered a vehicle in the eyes of the law and you're obliged to follow the road rules, the same as a car. Why didn't you stop?'

I had a feeling he wasn't going to like my answer.

'I don't have any brakes,' I said.

'You don't have any brakes,' he said.

'Well, I have brakes,' I said. 'They're just . . . not on the bike.'

'Not on the bike,' he said.

I nodded.

He thought about this for a while. 'Why aren't they on the bike?' he asked.

'It's a bit of a long story,' I said.

He looked at me, and then at his watch. And then back at me.

'Well you know what?' he said. 'I haven't got anywhere else to be in a hurry. Unless someone gets stabbed, and considering where we are, that might not be long. Failing that, I haven't got anywhere to be and nor does Probationary

Constable Williams here, so why don't you tell me the story? My name is Senior Constable Mark Wilcox, by the way.'

I explained about fixies and hills and stopping and bike polo and pizza boxes and orange chains.

'I see,' he said when I'd finished. 'You understand not having brakes makes your bicycle illegal. I see you haven't got a bell or reflectors either.'

I gazed at the bike, and pretended to look surprised, as if this was news to me.

'Is this your dog?'

'No,' I said. He had finished with the pizza box and was licking pear cider off my shoe now.

'Well he seems to like you. Are you sure it's not your dog?'

I said it wasn't my dog. 'I think it lives over there,' I said, pointing to the house. Senior Constable Wilcox followed my finger. He nodded.

'Have you got some ID on you?'

I gave him my driver's licence. He checked it over and handed it to Probationary Constable Williams, who took it into the car and started typing things into the computer.

'Have you ever been in trouble with the police before, Mr Granfield?'

I said I hadn't. He liked this answer.

'Mr Granfield, do you own an approved bicycle helmet?'

I told him I did. He asked where it was. I said it was under my bed. He indicated it wasn't likely to be as useful to me in its current location as it would be if it were on my head. He took the opportunity to point out that it was illegal to ride a bicycle in Queensland without an approved, correctly fitted and fastened bicycle helmet, and asked me if I was aware of that. I said I was aware of that.

Probationary Constable Williams came out of the car and handed me my licence back. He nodded to Senior Constable Wilcox.

'All right, Mr Granfield,' Senior Constable Wilcox said. 'Today is your lucky day.'

It didn't feel very lucky.

'I don't want to have to do all the paperwork, so I'm going to give you a choice. You can have drinking in public, failing to stop at an indicated stop sign or being in charge of a bicycle without an approved helmet. You're lucky you didn't crash into a traffic unit or they would have thrown the book at you.' He raised his eyebrow at me. 'Which would you like?'

I asked which one was best.

'They're all the same fine,' he said, 'but drinking in public isn't a traffic offence. I'd go with no helmet.'

'I'll take no helmet then,' I said.

He wrote me a ticket.

The Rottweiler had moved onto the ground now. He was nudging my foot. I shuffled my feet a bit and winced at the pain in my ankle.

'Have you got far to go?' Senior Constable Wilcox asked.

'Why? Do you want to give me a lift?' I asked.

'No, I can't. If I get called to an emergency and I have to throw some idiot in the back I can't have you complaining because he fiddled with your bike.'

'What if I promised not to complain?' I asked.

He pursed his lips and it looked like he was considering it. I think he felt bad leaving me hobbling around on the wrong side of the tracks. Before he could answer, though, something came over the police radio that sounded important. I think I heard the word 'homicide'. Although it could just have easily been 'gone inside'. I pretended it was homicide, and had visions of them bundling me into the car on the way to a shoot-out. 'All right,' I imagined Senior Constable Wilcox saying. 'We're a man down and you look like you know how to shoot. Grab this shotgun and cover me. Things could get nasty. Here, put this flak jacket on in case.'

He didn't though, he just said, 'We have to go,' and then told me that if he saw me riding around with no helmet on again he'd charge me with vandalism for the scratch I put on the car.

And with that they left in a blaze of lights and sirens.

The Rottweiler looked at me, perhaps apologetically, and then trotted back home, a little wobblier, but significantly less foamy than before. I waited until the police car was well out of sight, then sat down, opened the only cider that wasn't broken and sculled it. It helped the pain a little, but my ankle was still killing me so there was no way I was going to be pedalling my way to glory on National Bike Courier Bike Polo Championships Day now.

As I was considering my options a couple of other fixie riders came whooshing down the road. They looked the part with aero wheels on the front, cards woven in the back spokes and rolled up skinny jeans. Just like in the

Bicycle Film Festival videos. I guessed they were on the way to the park.

They saw me sitting in the gutter looking worse for wear and came over to see if I was all right.

'Hey, are you OK?' one asked.

'Yeah, just had a run in with the fuzz is all,' I said. They nodded respectfully. 'Are you guys heading to the bike polo nationals thing?'

'Yeah,' one said. 'Thought we'd go have a look.'

'Oh, you're not competing?' I asked.

They looked at me as if I'd just casually requested some fellatio. 'What, are you kidding?' the other one said.

'What do you mean?' I asked.

'The polo crew just go there to smash their bikes up. It's a bit of fun, I guess.' He looked down at his bike. 'But I just spent a hundred and fifty bucks sand-blasting and painting the frame, I don't want some psycho with a mallet hacking at it.'

He looked at my bike and saw the chips on the cross bar.

'Oh sorry, I didn't mean to be rude. I wasn't saying that if you were off to play polo you were a psycho or anything.'

'Oh, no, no,' I said. 'That just happened then: it hit the police car.'

'Ouch.'

'So, bike polo then,' I asked. 'Is that a bit frowned upon in purist circles?'

They thought about this.

'Well, it's not that it's frowned upon,' the first guy said. 'It's just that, your bike should be an extension of your personality. If your personality is whacking people with sticks, then bike polo is going to be right up your alley. I just prefer to express myself a little differently. Why do you ask, anyway?'

'Oh, I'm just new to this whole thing,' I said. 'I've only just got into single-speed bikes really.'

They thought this was cool.

'So what's the, like, ultimate fixie then?' I asked.

They had a think.

'Well, it's about who you are,' the second guy said. 'I've got a mate who's a tattoo artist and he's done up a design for his bike and he's drawing the design on the frame in tattoo ink. That's pretty cool.'

'No, wait.' The first guy laughed. 'Get this, OK, so I've got this mate, he likes to knit—total fucking hipster—he's made a scarf for his handlebars. It sounds weird, but it's pretty cool. It's all different colours, actually looks wicked.'

'So you reckon that's the ultimate fixie then?' I asked.

He thought about it for a bit longer.

'Absolutely, I think. Forget bike polo.' He laughed again. 'If you want the ultimate fixie, knit it a scarf.'

I pulled out my iPhone and wrote down a note. *Bike scarf.*

'Are you heading up to the park?' the second guy asked.

I thought about it. 'Nah, actually. I've got a website to build this afternoon.'

CHAPTER 14
THE HIPSTERNET

Scrabble is the reigning hipster board game of choice and it's easy to see why. The tiles are made from wood, which makes them vintage, the typography is divine and playing requires just enough mathematics to add up easy numbers, so you look reasonably smart without having to use too much brainpower. You also get a chance to show off all the big words you learned reading paperback re-issues of classic novels. You can play it in a café, you can play it in a park, you can play it in the daytime, you can play it in the dark. If you get bored with the game you can just pull out the Superglue, stick the letters to Nanna's old rings and make yourself some rad jewellery, as we've already seen. As far as hipster games go, it's even better than 'pin the tail back on the fur cardi you found in the op shop last Saturday'.

The fact that Hasbro, the makers of Scrabble, sued a popular Facebook knock-off their product for breach of copyright seems to have had little effect on the popularity of the board game. Generally, when a large corporation files a lawsuit against a trendy indie website, hipsters will rally for the little guy. In the case of Napster they even went as far as getting Justin Timberlake to play him in a movie. But far from diminishing in popularity, Scrabble seems to be, if anything, getting cooler by the year. (Of course, playing on a proper vintage set doesn't benefit Hasbro in the least, so that might be part of the reason it works for hipsters.)

Given that no proper hipster could be considered true to the faith without holding the curatorship of at least one trendy indie website of his/her own, I had considered, for a time, setting up some sort of online homage to Scrabble. It didn't seem like a hard ask — and given that hipster websites, almost without fail, all fall into one of a small handful of categories, I figured it was just a matter of picking a genre and adding a Scrabble element.

The most obvious potential hipster website candidate was the 'I'm a twenty-something arts graduate blog'. Starting one of these was easy. All you had to do was choose a username on a blogging platform and keep a journal with your witty observations about life as a twenty-something arts graduate. Moaning about your shit job in an advertising agency was a particularly popular topic, as was taking pictures of food, discussing the latest developments in life as a new media professional and interviewing other twenty-something arts graduate bloggers about their blogs. The only problem was, twenty-something arts graduate blogs were so popular that 687 of my 688 Facebook friends already had them — including one friend who was an eighteen-month-old baby and one who was a stuffed monkey. The only one of my Facebook friends who didn't have a twenty-something arts graduate blog was my Aunty Susan, who had only just discovered social networking after her colon surgery and now insisted on adding a comment to every single one of my status updates with news of her recovery.

Twenty-something arts graduate blogs were therefore far too mainstream to be hip. I'd also done some Googling and found 8.7 million other Scrabble blogs already in existence. I had kind of been beaten to the punch.

The 'ironic picture tumblr' seemed like the next best choice then. You've probably seen them—all you do is collect a few dozen pictures of something quirky on the internet and then upload one of them to a website each day until you either run out of pictures, get bored, or get caught by your boss. Cats are quite popular, as are sites with pictures of people who could either be hipsters or Jesus. My favourite though, was a tumblr account which published nothing but official North Korean state media photographs of Kim Jong Il looking at things. It had been going for more than a year and the curator still hadn't run out of material—surely I could find another loveable evil dictator who had a penchant for the word game and show photos of him bagging triple word scores. It didn't seem like such a stretch—Castro loved chess, Saddam Hussein was apparently mad for a game of poker—maybe Gaddafi loved Scrabble.

I did some searching but I couldn't really find any pictures of famous people playing Scrabble. I did, though, find a hoard of old photographs of Fidel Castro and Che Guevara at the 1966 Havana Chess Olympiad, which got me excited. They had two of the hippest bushranger beards I'd ever seen, so I started up a website called chesshipsters.com and posted pictures of them on it to see what would happen. I expected it to go viral within hours. When I ran out of pictures of Fidel I found a bunch of other retro-looking chess grand masters with thick-rimmed glasses and put them up. When I ran out of them I put up images of French artist and chess devotee Marcel Duchamp playing against naked chicks in the name of art. That got me up to nine posts and then I ran out of pictures of cool people playing chess so I abandoned the site. It ended up getting about eighty-eight visitors in total.

I decided to give up on the Scrabble idea altogether and concentrate on cats. Cats were a sure-fire route to becoming an internet sensation. I figured if I could compile a never-before-seen series of cats doing something cute, or strange, or better still, cute *and* strange, I would be onto a winner. Sure enough, a Google image search for 'cute kitten' revealed about 2.5 million results. There were pictures of kittens and every other object known to man, both animate and inanimate—kittens with ducks, kittens with balls of wool, kittens with bricks, and there, on page 32 of the Google Images search results was a picture of a cute little kitten holding a gun. Bingo.

To make sure I could find as many similar images as possible I pulled out a thesaurus and Googled 'kitten gun', 'cat gun', 'kitty revolver', 'cat rifle' and a few other variations—including, absent-mindedly, 'pussy gun', which seemed like a good idea at the time, but required a great deal of frantic back-button clicking and explaining when I noticed my neighbour was watering the garden outside and could see my screen. I did eventually find more than a dozen pictures of felines with firearms though. Kittenswithguns. com was available, but it was a bit too mainstream, so I registered kittehswithguns.com instead and set up the site with a new image every day for two weeks. It was about as popular as syphilis.

The problem was, I had been going for the easy options. Even if I had managed to become a viral internet sensation with some pictures of cats, it wasn't very hip. If I was to go down in hipstery as running the ultimate hipster website, I would have to aim higher. I realised I would have tackle one of the two granddaddies of the hipsternet: The 'Music You Haven't Heard of Reviews Website', or the 'Amateur Photography Community'.

Starting a 'Music You Haven't Heard of Reviews Website' had potential. It wouldn't be too hard to set up, but it would also take years of intense cyber-bullying and late nights huddled over my laptop reviewing shit music no one had heard of. With the exception of Thursday nights, when I would have to go *out* to venues and stay up *all* night listening to shit music no one had heard of—no band popular enough to get a gig on a Friday or Saturday night could possibly be worth listening to. I didn't much like that idea though. Running such a website would also require a lot of time, effort, talent and dedication—four things any hipster worth his salt had none of.

If I was to truly become a hero of the hipsternet I would need to employ myself in the practice of a pursuit that took no time, effort, dedication or talent whatsoever.

Amateur photography, it seemed, would be perfect.

Starting an amateur photography community was not, of course, enough in itself. There were already plenty of amateur photography communities out there. Hipsters love amateur photography, but if I was going to have the ultimate hipster website I needed something much bigger and better. I needed to marry amateur photography with another ultimate hipster pursuit. Bike polo had left a bitter taste in my mouth. And there were already more than enough music websites in the world. Fashion had potential, but I needed more than just a fashion photography website.

It suddenly dawned on me that there was one thing hipsters love more than bike polo, amateur photography and fashion put together. Above all other things, hipsters love anonymously judging people who aren't as cool as them. If I could build an amateur fashion photography community where hipsters could anonymously criticise everyone else, it would surely be the world's most super-ultimate hipster website ever.

It was genius, but the website wasn't going to build itself. I knew enough new media developers to put together some sort of online system where people could upload pictures and let other people say how much they liked or hated them, but I needed a bunch of amateur fashion photos to get the ball rolling. I couldn't ask Hipster Radio Station Ex-Girlfriend for her stash and I didn't really know any other amateur fashion photographers. If I was going to make my website dream a reality I would have to become an amateur fashion photographer myself.

The only problem was, I didn't know anything about amateur fashion photography.

I needed to get myself into a course. And I didn't have a whole lot of time. Or money.

If I was going to start the world's ultimate online amateur fashion photography community, and become chief judge and photographer, I needed to quickly become at one with the lens. To do that, I needed a teacher. More than a teacher, I needed a guide, a yogi—a brilliant leader with decades of experience who was willing to pass his or her knowledge on to me as disciple.

Not finding anyone who even remotely met that description in the Yellow Pages, I settled for Alan, who, according to his ad, did mostly baby portraits and weddings. He was offering two-for-one prints with the purchase of every shoot and, as luck would have it, also conducted digital SLR workshops every Saturday morning from ten am to two pm at his studio, which happened to be a quick, flat bike ride across town from my house.

Alan didn't sound very yogi-like, but he was fabulously convenient.

I sent Alan an e-mail asking whether or not there were any places in the next workshop (in two days' time) and received an answer back within the hour. It seemed I was in luck—not only was Alan particularly convenient, he was also spectacularly available. He was also rather cheap—the four-hour course only cost $80. He might not have been Annie Leibowitz, but he certainly seemed like good value. And he took Visa.

I was in.

As it turned out, Alan may not have *been* Annie Leibowitz, but he certainly was something of a fan. He'd met her once at an exhibition in New York. She'd signed his lens cap with a silver pen and he'd had it framed. It was hanging on the wall in the foyer of the studio next to some pictures of babies and a panoramic photograph of the Brooklyn Bridge at night.

I was the first student to arrive.

I didn't really want to lie to him, but the truth wasn't going to make much sense, so I told Alan I was there because I'd always been interested in photography, that my friends said I took pretty good photos and that I seemed to have a bit of a knack for it but that I'd never studied it or anything, so I wanted to learn some of the more technical aspects.

He nodded a lot and said that was 'great'. I told him I was particularly interested in fashion photography and was thinking about taking photos of fashionable people I met on the street in Brooklyn. He asked me if I was from Brooklyn because I didn't sound like I was from Brooklyn and pointed to the bridge photo on the wall. He asked me if I spent a lot of time over there.

I said I had been to New York once a few years ago and that I thought it was 'great'. He said that was great. Then there was some silence so I looked at baby photos on the wall.

'Are any of the children yours?' I asked. He told me they weren't—he'd only just got married a few months earlier and there were no plans just yet.

I told him about a website I saw once where you could send a woman in Texas photos from your eight-year-old daughter's beauty pageants and she would use Photoshop to put lipstick and make-up on them to make them look prettier. I asked him if he used Photoshop much and if we'd be learning about that today. He said that today was more about using the camera but that he ran an editing course once a month that I could come to if I liked: it was $150. I said I'd think about it.

'So where's your rig?' he asked, looking at the bicycle-messenger-style bag I'd salvaged from the market stall and then at my hat.

I had a trucker cap on because I wanted to look like Spike Lee, because he was handy with a camera and I figured Spike Lee would be a pretty good vibe to channel, and for a second I thought he might have thought I had a trucker cap on because I drove a big rig, but I followed his gaze to my bag and realised he was talking about the camera I would be using in the class.

I pulled my iPhone out of my pocket, put it on the glass coffee table and nodded. 'It's got a five-megapixel lens,' I told him. 'There's a couple of apps I've been using: do you know Hipstamatic?'

He chuckled.

'No, serious,' he said. 'Are you a Nikon or a Canon man?'

He was looking expectantly at the bag again.

I told him I wasn't sure and asked which one was better. He told me it was personal preference and that he was a Nikon man, always had been, but that if I had a Canon it was OK, he wouldn't judge me, I just wouldn't be allowed to take the course. He chuckled at this too. I made a $500 bet with myself that he told that joke every single week.

There was a bit of a pause.

'I was just going to use my iPhone, hey,' I said.

He looked at the bag again and said 'Really?' in the same tone of voice you'd use if a stranger sat down next to you on a long-haul flight, introduced themselves, ran through the usual weather chat and then told you their doctor had recently informed them there was an eighty per cent chance they no longer had leprosy but they were off to your destination city for some specialist tests which were more accurate.

I nodded.

He guessed that would be OK, he supposed.

I showed him some pictures on my iPhone that I'd taken of my friend's sister wearing a blue 1950s dress and pearls and told him I was going to put them on a fashion website I was putting together. I'd added retro Polaroid borders to them all. He said they were 'great' but his voice sounded a little more distant this time.

Luckily, at that point a group of other students walked in and Alan introduced himself. It turned out they were real estate agents from a big office who had been sent by their boss to learn how to take better property photos. They'd all just recently earned their real estate agent licences and were full of the exuberance I imagine would come at the beginning of a long and profitable career getting up early on weekends to sell terrace houses to lawyers who liked to do crosswords in their spare time. They were sharing the two real estate agency Nikons, which Alan said was a 'good solid camera'. When he started out, he said, he used the model just up from that one. It had a number and a letter in it but I forget which ones.

Michelle turned up next; she was a blonde hippie chick who was studying journalism at uni but she was into photography and was thinking about switching to fine arts, but wanted to see how she went doing a couple of courses outside uni first. She had a Nikon something. Alan liked her.

Jodie arrived just after her. She had been a model for a while but was starting to get into fashion photography a bit more. She had a fancy-looking Canon, a super-cute 1950s-style floral dress, light blue Doc Martens and some vintage thick-rimmed reading glasses. I shuffled over on the couch a bit more so there was room for her and she thanked me. I privately wondered if she was a fan of Spike Lee but I didn't say anything.

There was some small talk about how rainy it had been lately and people asked polite questions about the photos on the wall that Alan was happy to answer.

Wayne came in five minutes late and apologised but traffic had been pretty bad. Wayne was a pastry chef who wanted to be a food photographer. Wayne needed to lay off the pies.

Alan clapped his hands together once as Wayne found a chair, said 'OK!' with more than sufficient gusto and told us a bit about himself. It turned out he was a not-particularly-talented baby-portrait photographer who didn't have much of a head for business so he was running cheap photography courses on the side after hours to help pay the rent for a studio lease he couldn't really afford. He didn't put it quite like that though. His version included more mention of helicopters and Annie Leibowitz.

We then took it in turns to tell the group about ourselves and what photographers we liked and why we got into photography. We had to describe our level of photography knowledge on a scale of one to ten and most people said two or three, except Wayne, who said seven. We had a camera show and tell and everyone thought I was joking when I said I was using my iPhone and they looked at my bag, but then they realised I was serious and it was awkward for a few moments until Alan gave us all an A4 booklet which was the manual for the course.

The topics were as follows:

- Introduction
- A history of DSLR
- The DSLR system
- Getting to grips with your DSLR
- Seeing the picture
- Landscapes
- Nature
- People
- Babies
- Architecture
- Still life

- Action
- Getting more from your DSLR

And there was a copyright notice and Alan's name. Alan had the same last name as a famous actor and he made a joke about it but only Wayne found it funny.

I had a feeling the topics with 'DSLR' in them were probably going to go over my head, but felt for sure I was going to be the star student in the 'people' section. I'd been studying fashion blogs all afternoon in preparation.

I kind of zoned out for a while when all the acronyms were going on but when we go to the 'seeing the picture' part of the course Alan started getting a bit more excited. He asked us to gather round.

'Guys,' he said. 'I'm going to show you something which will change the way you look at photographs forever. It's called the rule of thirds.'

Apparently an ancient Greek mathematician photographer named Euclid came up with a theory that if you divide photographs into thirds and then align your subject at the intersection of two of those thirds it would look better. Da Vinci used the same principle when he painted. Michelangelo used it when he sculpted. I didn't quite understand, but I wrote the name 'Euclid' down in my Moleskine notebook anyway, in case it was no longer considered a proper noun and I could use it in a game of Scrabble one day.

I asked Alan if the rule of thirds had anything to do with triangles. It didn't.

He demonstrated how the rule of thirds worked by getting Michelle to stand in front of one of those curvy white walls with no corners. He took one shot where she wasn't lined up with anything in particular and showed us. It looked pretty bad. He then turned on a set of three rows in the viewfinder of his camera and lined her eyes up with the top row. I wasn't really into hippie chicks or mathematicians, but I had to admit she looked much better. Euclid was onto something. Armed with this knowledge I had a feeling I would be the world's premier amateur fashion photographer within hours.

Alan talked about foregrounds and backgrounds and lighting for a while and then we had to practise taking pictures of buildings. He said the light was a bit harsh now and that the best time to shoot architecture was around sunset. When we got to the still life section we had to shoot a vase on a table. I asked Alan why there weren't any flowers in the vase. He said it wasn't important and to just focus on the vase. I thought this was lame but didn't say so. The vase was triangular though, which I thought was pretty cool.

The 'action' section was a bit more fun—we had to pair up and take pictures of each other running through the studio and try and blur the background but keep the subject in focus by changing the ISO setting. I didn't have an ISO setting, so I cued up some Austrian dubstep on my iPhone and asked Jodie to run in time with the music hoping that by judging what the beat was doing, I could tell where she was going to be and arrange the shot around that. It didn't work at all so I just added a blue filter and a border and that seemed to fix things up. She thought it was pretty funny.

At the end of the course when we'd finished taking our photos we all had to download them to a computer with a giant screen and Alan talked us through what he liked about them. The consensus was that my framing was good. Jodie liked my Polaroid borders. Alan reckoned if I bought a decent rig I'd probably be able to come up with some great shots. He said he had an old Nikon body for sale and I could have it for $450 if I wanted. I said I'd think about it.

I felt like I'd learned a lot, but there was a hell of a lot of work to do now if I was going to get my amateur fashion photography community up and running. I had a couple of photos of Jodie to get me started but I needed rather a lot more if I was going to get any traction. I couldn't start a community with two pictures of a girl running in time to Austrian dubstep, no matter how cute or hip she was.

As we were leaving I decided to hit her up for more.

'Hey, Jodie,' I asked.

She turned around. 'Yep?'

'I was wondering, and I know you're probably busy and everything, but I'm keen to get into a bit of fashion photography myself, I know you were a model and all, do you reckon I could practise by taking some photos of you?' I said a silent little prayer hoping she'd say yes. 'I love your glasses by the way,' I added.

She smiled. 'That sounds like fun! When were you thinking?'

I hadn't planned that far ahead.

'Oh, umm, well, let me see.' I mentally checked my schedule. I had nothing on at all for the next week and

I hadn't been on a date since Hipster Radio Station Ex-Girlfriend Dumped Me. If I was smart enough I could potentially kill two birds with one stone. 'I'm a bit busy at the moment,' I said. 'But, well, how about next Saturday afternoon? Around sunset I guess, like Alan taught us. The light should be pretty good then. We could go down by the river. There's a cool bar there with some great brickwork. It would make a nice backdrop.'

'OK, that would be great. You can buy me a beer afterwards as payment.'

There was, indeed, a God.

'Also, and it's totally OK if you're not cool, but I'm starting this little fashion community thing and I was kind of hoping I could put the pics up on the web. Do you reckon that would be OK? It's just a little thing I'm starting, kind of a fashion community thing.'

'Oh, really.' She was turning her nose up a bit and frowning. I'd gone too far. 'Yeah, I'm not sure about that,' she said. 'Don't know if I'd be comfortable with it. It's not like I'm still a model or anything.'

I nodded. 'Hey, that's totally fine, I'm—'

'I'm kidding, you douche!' she interrupted. 'Of course. It sounds great. What sort of fashion community is it?'

This was exciting—she seemed genuinely interested.

'Well, it's an amateur fashion photography community where people upload their images and members of the community can rate them and tell the world whether they like them or not. So, if they think the outfit and the photo is cool they just click a button and it registers it as a vote.

Sam studying some hipster chord changes.

George taking a break from drum duty in TRI△NGLR.

Before the indie folk songs turned into Korean punk songs.

Jake getting a bit louder than I was expecting in the studio.

Trixie the Fixie arriving in a box.

Taking Trixie for a cruise down to a local hipster watering hole.

On the way
to practise for
the National
Bike Courier
Bicycle Polo
Championships.

If there's one thing
hipsters do better
than anyone, it's
chilling in the park.

Sunset is the new dawn.

Fixies aren't that common in Brisbane, so when I saw another one, I snapped it.

My first digital
SLR iPhone
camera shot of
Jodie.

Jodie, posing for
the hipster camera.

I was trying to get Jodie to run in time to the music.

It didn't work.

Jodie and I being hip in a café.

Coffee #1.

After coffee #6 and
starting to feel a
little worse
for wear.

The more people that like something, the higher it gets rated—and vice versa.'

She was nodding. 'So, like Lookbook?'

'What do you mean?' I asked.

'Lookbook.'

I shrugged.

'It's an amateur fashion photography site. A bit like, well, pretty similar to, kind of, what you just said.'

'Oh.'

She smiled. 'It's pretty mainstream now though. It's all just wannabe kids from Asia. You don't want to do that. I'm sure your idea is much cooler.'

'Yeah, no, mine's a bit different,' I said. 'It's got, umm, no, well, to be honest that was my idea. What's it called again?'

'Lookbook. You should check it out. Hey, we should upload a photo from Saturday to it.'

'Yeah?'

She said yeah.

'Hey,' she said. 'Are you hungry?'

'Yeah, starving actually. I could eat a horse.'

'Eew. Well, I'm vegan, so no horses, but I know a great little vegetarian café near here; do you want to go get something to eat?' She looked at my ring. 'They've got a Scrabble board—we can play.'

'Sure.'

'Is vegetarian OK?'

I looked at her. She was gorgeous. And hip. Very hip. Potentially *ultimate hipster girlfriend* hip.

'Actually,' I said. 'That would be perfect. I'm actually a vegetarian too.'

'Really! That's awesome.' She looked surprised. And delighted. 'How long have you been a vegetarian?'

CHAPTER 15
VEGETARIANISM

There are three reasons why people choose to be vegetarians. The first is because they have a moral objection to eating animals. The second is for medical reasons. The third is because they're trying to impress a girl.

I wasn't lying when I told Jodie I was a vegetarian. Technically the definition of a vegetarian is someone who doesn't eat meat. Admittedly I had eaten a bacon sandwich for breakfast, but I was planning on having leftover risotto for dinner and that had no protein in it at all. The fridge at home contained nothing but a few orphaned beers and some cheese and I didn't know what I was having for breakfast the next day, so for all intents and purposes, at that point in time I *technically* was a vegetarian.

Up until quite recently, breakfast time in fact, I had been of the opinion that unless someone with a stethoscope and a Mercedes reliably informed you that digesting the flesh of another beast would leave you dead, or at the very least, convulsing with a significant degree of gusto, you had no plausible reason for not eating meat.

Now, I was as environmentally-conscious as the next guy—I'd seen Xavier Rudd in a carpark in Torquay once, I'd been to Nimbin twice and I'd been in a Toyota Prius three times—so I got that it was wrong to eat dolphin burgers.

I got that some people avoided chickens which have been kept in pens the size of matchboxes and injected with enough hormones to make a Chinese swimmer change sexes and then change back again. I even got that Hindus don't like eating bovines on the grounds that they may be gods. If I shared their belief, I too would have been willing to give cows the benefit of the doubt—I've been chowing down on Big Macs my entire life, it would have sucked to finally get to heaven and realise the pearly gates are attached to an electric fence guarding a deity named Daisy.

I got all those reasons, and I was happy to avoid eating dolphins and whales and mentally-ill poultry and anything in a can, and anything you'd put on a leash and take for a walk to the park, and anything exceptionally cute, fatty, furry or smart enough to learn sign-language. But that still left a veritable ark of wildlife on the lunch list.

Ducks, with their dim-witted quacking and gregarious shitting, are one of the most annoying creatures on the planet; if ducks disappeared from the food chain the only noticeable impact on the planet would be an over-abundance of stale bread crusts. Obviously I'm not advocating their extinction—they're too delicious to do away with altogether—but if a few went missing every now and then and ended up in my curry, I had no complaints.

Sheep, of course, are cute for a while. No one is happy to let a lamb suffer, but once they get old and woolly their existence consists almost exclusively of erroneous trotting and bleating. If a sheep, I thought, got lost, waddled into an abattoir and fell on my plate, well, bad luck, Dolly. And prawns? Nobody, not even People for the Ethical Treatment of Animals, not even Michael Moore, gave a toss about prawn welfare. Prawns were the rats of the sea as far as I was concerned—tiny, innumerable little poo-eating exoskeletal pockets of delicious.

But Jodie had, in the bat of an eyelash, caused me to rethink my meat manifesto. Maybe there was more to lunch than ham, more to dinner than lamb and more to breakfast than bacon. After thirty years of meat-eatin', my digesty-bits could probably use a little sweepin'. I'd once moved states for a girl—surely moving my bowels wasn't too hard a task.

At the end of the day, though, it wasn't a question for the heart: it was a matter for the hip. I hadn't considered what the ultimate hipster food pyramid should look like, only that it should be triangular in shape and have heirloom tomatoes at its base.

When I thought about it, though, there were quite a number of reasons why I *couldn't* be the ultimate hipster and still eat a lot of meat.

The first and most obvious is that supermarkets are unequivocally mainstream. Organic fruit and vegetables, with their imperfections and home-grown origins, are the ultimate expression of alt and should form the bulk of any hipster diet. A true hipster should either buy her groceries from an independent health food store or, even better, eat from his own veggie garden. In the same way that knitting a scarf is far cooler than buying one, the logical conclusion is that if you haven't got a cow in the backyard, you shouldn't be eating steak.

And while seeking out alternative ways of existing is obviously a core lifestyle principle of hipsterdom, at the end of the day, choosing a home-grown rockmelon over a cantaloupe genetically modified in China isn't a life or death matter. Sadly though, in the twenty-first century, hipsters have a far graver reason to be keeping their eating habits closer to home.

Whereas our parents were brought up fearing communism, our generation is terrified of carbon dioxide. While the cool baby boomers grew up in fear of nuclear war between America and Russia, any indie kid born since 1980 has had to live with the pressing concern that in the not-too-distant future sea levels may suddenly rise and render the backyard of their dad's waterfront investment property useless for Ultimate Frisbee. Since food production and manufacturing and transport logistics are major contributors to climate change, true hipsters don't let anything pass their lips if it has travelled more than a few hours to get to their plate.

Cattle are an equally evil climate change culprit. Methane is over twenty times more effective in trapping atmospheric heat than carbon dioxide and a single cow blows enough gas out of its arse each year to melt an iceberg the size of Greenland. These gassy emissions, combined with the disastrous effect clearing farmland has on native forests, make grazing animals environmental enemy number one. Any hipster eating meat is effectively sanctioning global warming. Global warming isn't cool.

The third, and most compelling reason why the ultimate hipster should be vegetarian is that vegetarianism is, like, *totally* in right now. The greatest hipsters in history, from

Aristotle to Allen Ginsberg, have all avoided meat and it's a trend that has only gained momentum over time. The hippest cafés in the hippest cities have extensive vegetarian options or, better still, are completely vegan. Eating a chicken burger at an Animal Collective gig is as culturally insensitive as fucking a pig in a synagogue.

I was mulling all these thoughts over when Jodie waved her hand in front of my face to get my attention.

'Matt?' She was looking at me funny. 'Hello. How long have you been a vegetarian?'

'Oh,' I said. 'All my life really—on and off. I don't think we have a choice in this world really if we want it to be sustainable.'

She was nodding.

'I mean, sure, if I'm starving and stuck on a desert island and there's nothing to eat but a kebab and it's a choice of that or dying, then I'll eat the kebab. In fact I've had a few near-death experiences after eating kebabs, but as a rule, I'm pretty against eating meat. You know what I mean?'

She did. She knew exactly what I meant. She knew what I meant so much she linked her arm in mine and walked with me like that all the way to the café. Her little blue Doc Martens clomping merrily along the footpath, carefully avoiding any ants which might happened to have crossed her path.

'So, how long have you been a vegan?' I asked.

I forget the name of the café now but it's not important. It could have been any hipster coffee shop in any hipster city in the world. The chairs were milk crates with cushions. The menu was written in chalk. The milk next to the coffee machines was all soy, the beans were all organic fair trade. There were socialist postcards in a rack next to a stack of arts and entertainment supplements from left-leaning newspapers and street press magazines. The sport and finance sections had been removed in case they offended anyone. The waitresses had tattoos and fringes and frowns. The waiters had a demeanour and fashion sense that suggested they were dependent on methadone, even if their haircuts had clearly cost more than a small farm in Moldova.

It was two-thirty in the afternoon but all present looked like they'd just got out of bed and they were all clearly hungover. Everyone would have been smoking if they were allowed, especially the lone guy up the back writing on his MacBook, but they were not, so they weren't. Obviously no one was eating bacon but the only menu they had out was for breakfast. There probably wasn't any other type of menu.

It was enticing. I chained Trixie up to a lamppost and we snagged a spot upstairs by the window in the sun.

'I love this place,' Jodie confessed. 'The beans are to die for. You should get the beans. Or the quinoa pilaf. The quinoa pilaf is amazing.'

Quinoa pilaf sounded like it might turn into an South American dictator at any second, so I ordered the beans. Broad beans spooning each other around a plate with baked eggs, tomato, pecorino and white truffle oil along for the ride. I hadn't eaten a broad bean since I was six. Dad used to grow them in the vege garden at home and Mum would boil them until they resembled hommus. These were crisp and sweet and delicious. The vegetarians obviously knew something Mum didn't. I took a photo and immediately posted it to the internet—partly for posterity, mostly so I had an excuse to tag Jodie and add her as a friend on Facebook.

We started a game of Scrabble.

'So what have you got on this weekend?' I asked.

'Well, I had roller derby last night,' she replied, 'so I'm a bit sore.' She showed me some complex-looking bruises on her elbows; they included all three primary colours. 'And I was going to go see a movie this evening with a friend—*Fremde Haut*—I've been wanting to see it for ages but never had time.'

'What's it about?' I asked.

'Ah, it's a German film about an Iranian refugee. She moves to a small town, has to disguise herself as a man and ends up falling in love with a local girl. It's a bit of an identity crisis flick. Won lots of awards though.'

I nodded. 'Your move.'

She played the word 'ignorant' by putting the 'i' over a 'd' to make 'id'.

'I was watching a German film the other day,' I said.

'Oh yes, which one?'

'Ah, I can't remember the title. Similar theme though.'

'Mm. Good?'

'Yeah. It wasn't the most complex plot.'

Jodie nodded. 'Was that at the queer film festival down at the Dendy?'

The waitress, whose nose ring was glinting in the afternoon sun, interrupted the conversation to collect our plates. 'Coffee, guys?' she asked. We both said no. Jodie had already had two that day. Caffeine gave me a headache so I ordered a green tea with jasmine.

'She was cute, wasn't she?' Jodie said after the waitress left.

I turned around to look again. She was.

'So,' Jodie started, 'I was thinking: the light is starting to fade a bit already, what are you doing right now? Should we go and take some pics? You're cute. You'd be a good model. Finish your tea and let's go.'

'Oh, I was going to ... actually. Yes.' Who was I kidding? I had nothing on at all, other than a date with Claire the flatmate's cat and some online German cinematography if we both got lonely.

'I've never modelled before,' I said. 'I mean, I've done band photos and things, but not, like, properly.'

'It'll be fun!' she assured me. 'Besides, we're both professional photographers now. And I want to get some action shots of you on your bike in this light.'

She had a point.

'My framing is better than yours though,' I said, unchaining Trixie.

Jodie laughed. 'Is that a lame bicycle joke?'

I hadn't thought about that. 'No. You want to hear one though?'

'Sure.' I paid the bill and we headed off on our way.

'So there's this cyclist riding a tandem bicycle along a country road, he's got a worried look on his face, which gets even worse when a police car pulls up in front of him and tells him to pull over. "Hey, mate," the police officer says. "You're in a lot of trouble. Didn't you realise your wife fell off the back about a mile ago? I almost hit her." "Oh thank God," says the cyclist. "I thought I'd gone deaf."'

Jodie looked at me. 'Yeah, that's pretty lame.'

'Cute though,' I said.

Jodie pointed out that it wasn't very cute for the wife. I said she was probably in better condition than if she'd been at roller derby. She punched me in the ribs. I had to pretend it didn't hurt.

It was almost four-thirty by the time we got to the park. The light was indeed fading, but the trees made for some interesting shadows, which we darted in and out of. There was a light breeze picking up and I got a gorgeous photo of Jodie pulling the hair out of her eyes as her dress billowed slightly and she squinted into the sun.

She thought it was great. 'You do have good framing,' she said. 'Let me get one of you riding with the sun behind you. Go over there and ride towards me, quickly.'

I cycled off into the middle distance and came cruising past. She took a shot.

'Nah, you're going to have to take it a bit faster,' she said.

'I want it to all be a bit of a blur as you sail past and I'm going to try and get just you in focus. And look past me, is if I'm not supposed to be here.'

We had another crack.

She looked pleased this time. I rode back up and she was looking at the viewfinder. 'Check this out!' It was a lovely photo. My scarf was billowing behind me like I was the Wicked Witch of the West caught in a tornado.

'OK, my turn,' I said. 'I want one of you with the sun behind you just as it's almost ready to go behind the horizon. Not on the bike or anything, just, kind of gazing, and it'll be all washed out. My ex used to do that in every freaking photo. It's all the rage apparently.'

Jodie put her back to the sun and did a model pout.

'Was your ex a photographer?' she asked.

I snapped away. 'Sort of. Hey, stop pouting. You look like a model. I mean, that's a good thing, but just look like you're having a nice time.'

'I am having a nice time,' she said with a smile. 'So what happened with your ex? If you don't mind me asking.' She checked a text message on her mobile.

'I don't mind you asking. It's a bit of a long story though.'

She asked for the nutshell version.

'Well, in a nutshell, she said she couldn't figure out who the real me was and said I didn't seem to know either. Her theory was that I was a different person depending on who I was hanging around with and that I needed to stop giving a shit what other people thought and just be true to myself.'

Jodie nodded. I captured a nice image of her looking concerned.

'How long ago was this?'

I told her it was about four months ago.

'Was she right?' she asked.

I took another photo of her, head cocked slightly to the side.

'Yeah, I guess. Who does know who they are, though, whatever that means?'

Jodie took a few steps closer.

'I'm not sure if she *was* right, you know. You seem pretty sure of yourself to me.'

'Oh yes?' I asked. Intrigued. 'What makes you say that?'

She looked me up and down. 'Well, you're clearly a bit of a hipster, for a start.'

'Just a *bit* of a hipster?'

'Well, I didn't want to be rude. You're about the biggest fucking hipster I've ever seen, but that's not a bad thing. You've got your look down. Your little vintage skater shoes, your designer flannelette shirt. Those jeans. That weird necklace. Those Buddy Holly glasses. I like that. I bet you listen to a lot of bands nobody has heard of.'

I wasn't quite sure what to say to that. It did sound like a compliment though.

'And the vegetarian thing, that's so honourable. I like that you care so much. It's rare to find a guy with such honest conviction.' She looked me in the eyes and squeezed my hand.

I nodded.

'Come here,' she said. 'Let's do a self portrait of both of

us.' She put an arm around my waist and put her cheek on mine, holding the camera out in front of us. Click.

It was a cute photo. The light was almost gone though.

'OK,' she said. 'I'm getting a bit chilly. I need to go home and change into something more comfortable. My place is just around the corner: do you want to come back for a coffee?' She put her arm in mine again and started leading me away. I didn't resist.

It was getting chilly, and dark, and I had no lights or reflectors on my bike, obviously, so I wasn't sure how I was going to get home without getting hit by a car, but it didn't matter. We walked in silence for a while, admiring the last remnants of the sunset as it faded gently into the horizon over the city. Jodie cuddled up a bit closer to keep warm.

'Hey,' I said. She looked up at me. 'I have a bit of a confession.'

'Oh really?' she said.

'Yeah. Umm. I don't really drink coffee. It kind of gives me a headache.'

She nodded. 'That's OK. I didn't really want a coffee anyway.' She squeezed my arm.

We kept walking for a while.

'And.' I was a bit nervous now. I'd been living a bit of a lie. 'I'm not actually . . . not *really* a vegetarian either. I mean, I am now, I've decided to turn vegetarian, but, yeah, I kind of wasn't before this afternoon.' I grimaced a bit—expecting the worst.

'Yeah, I know,' she said.

We stopped walking.

'What?' I said.

'I know you're not a vegetarian,' she said. 'You can't even pronounce vegan correctly. You keep saying vee-gun. It's vay-gun. It's OK, though,' she said. 'I think it's cute.'

'Aren't you angry I lied to you?' I asked.

'No, boys have said a lot worse to try and get in my pants before.' We started walking again.

'Oh, I wasn't trying to get in your pants,' I scoffed.

'Yes you were. Why are you coming back to my place for a coffee then? You don't even drink coffee and, putting that aside for a second, everyone knows that coffee after dark doesn't mean coffee anyway.'

She had me there.

'So what are you doing then, with the tape around your neck, with the becoming vegetarian on a whim, with the Buddy Holly glasses? Are those even real?'

'Yeah they're real. I need them to read.'

'The only thing you've read today is tea leaves.'

She had me again.

'Do you think your ex was right then?' she asked.

I thought about this.

'I think very few people actually spend any amount of time thinking about who they are. They just go through this life taking things as they come, adopting fashion trends as they come and go, listening to whatever music is on the radio, and then at a point, somewhere around thirty I guess, they hit the pause button and go: "OK, I'm sick of changing. This'll do—this haircut, these pants, this iPod playlist. I'm just going to stick with these for the rest of my life." Well, I kind of don't want to do that.'

She was looking at me now. Listening.

'So, I kind of got to a point where *I* said: "You know what? Rather than just hit pause, what if I threw everything into becoming a particular brand of person? What if I became the ultimate hipster for a while, just to see what would happen?" Just to see what I could learn.'

'And what have you learned?' she asked.

It was a good question.

'I don't know,' I admitted. 'But it's been fun pretending.'

She let that sink in. 'I'm not surprised,' she said. 'We're at my house now, by the way. I mean I'm not surprised you don't know what you've learned. Who you are is a lot more than your wardrobe and your taste in music and your bicycle.'

I nodded. Of course. We were walking up the path to her doorstep and she had her keys in her hand. There was a pair of roller skates on the porch.

'I'm really a bit disappointed in you, actually. I don't think you are serious about finding out who you are.'

I wasn't sure what to say to that, but I was pretty certain I'd blown my chances.

'Because if you were,' she continued, 'if you were serious about being the ultimate hipster, you'd be drinking a hell of a lot more coffee, you fucking pansy.' She smiled. 'Of all the hipster things you could do, I would have thought becoming a serious soy latte connoisseur would have been at the top of the list.'

Once again, she had me.

'I'd make you one, but I've only got instant shit. You can't start becoming a coffee drinker on Nescafé. Find a good barista to do introduce you to it properly. And take some Panadol with you when you go.'

I smiled.

'Do you want to come in?' she asked. 'My date for tonight cancelled on me; that was her texting me before. You can watch *Fremde Haut* with me if you like. You might learn something. It's pretty appropriate for you actually, given you're a cultural refugee.'

'Yeah, OK,' I said. 'Have you got a computer I can download these photos to first? I want to get them up on my blog.'

'Are you still going to do that?' she asked. 'I wouldn't bother if it was me. Wouldn't it be a far more hipster thing to do to just put up the site, Tweet about it for a couple of days and then just forget about it because it's all too hard?'

Yet another good point.

'How do you know so much about hipsters anyway?' I asked. 'You seem to know more than me.'

'Well, I was a model, but my day job is in an art gallery, and when I'm not doing that, I'm the curator of a queer film festival, so it's my job to know what's cool.'

'A queer film festival?' I asked. She nodded. This was disappointing. 'So I'm not going to be getting in your pants, am I?'

She smiled. 'Sorry, sweetheart. You're not my type.' I got a kiss on the cheek. 'I do think you're cute, though. You're also funny. And smart. Even if you do have a malfunctioning gaydar. I'm sure you'll make some girl very happy one day. As long as you be yourself.'

I thanked her.

'You don't have to start being yourself straight away though. I actually think it's cool you're trying to be someone else. It'll give you perspective. As will drinking a fuck tonne of coffee.'

I told her that might make me vomit.

'Vomiting gives you perspective too,' she said. 'And Matt?'

'Yes.'

'Your ex was full of shit. Only someone who was totally comfortable with who they are would wear pants that tight.'

CHAPTER 16
I DRINK SO MUCH COFFEE I GET HIGH

As the most widely-used psychoactive drug in the world, you'd think caffeine would be too mainstream for the cool kids. But you'd be wrong. It would seem that like breathing, eating and sleeping, drinking coffee is a human constant. It's also the world's best known cure for a hangover—and hipsters are always hungover.

Hipsters love their coffee. But only in the right incarnation and correct environment. The instant version is obviously a no-no. A true hipster's taste is far too discerning. Corporate coffee is also completely out of the question—Starbucks' ubiquity perfectly epitomises the soul-destroying homogeneity of mainstream popular culture that hipsters stand so indifferently steadfast against. On the other hand, the independent coffee and bookshops that provide outer-inner-city young folk with their daily stream of caffeine are the ultimate expression of individuality and rebellion.

If hydroponic cannabis is the gateway to heroin, organic rainforest alliance coffee is the gateway to hipsterdom. The dark, funky cafés of Surry Hills, Shoreditch, Brooklyn and Berlin are the closest thing hipsters have to a natural habitat. Jodie was right. If I was to become one with my subculture, I had to become one with its ecosystem — and its beverage preferences.

This was going to be more of a problem than you might think.

Brits and Australians go through about three kilograms of coffee per person each year. Scandinavians drink four times as much — it's dark and cold up there and clearly they need something to keep them awake. The average American coffee drinker has three cups a day. Your average hipster by comparison drinks more coffee than a long-haul Norwegian airline pilot with shares in the Vittoria factory.

I, on the other hand, go through three cups of coffee a year.

Coffee makes me dizzy. And it gives me a headache and heartburn. And if I have it after eight am I can't sleep until four am. And I have dreams about dragons. I can't even drink strong black tea. If I drank a Red Bull I would quite literally grow wings.

But I'd tattooed myself in the name of hipsterdom. I'd (almost) played polo with crazed drunken bicycle couriers. Becoming a coffee connoisseur and copping a few sleepless nights in the name of indie science was one of the least crazy things I was prepared to do on my quest for cool.

Given I couldn't taste the difference between the best café and Nescafé, I was going to need to enlist some help. I needed a coffee guide; a mentor; a soy latte sommelier. Someone with more caffeine in their blood than blood. I needed to find a barista who would make me as much of the dark stuff as I wanted with a disregard for my health and sanity so total it bordered on misdemeanour. More importantly, I needed someone who wouldn't sue me if I said their coffee machine put me in hospital.

As it turned out, I knew such a man. We also happened to share a set of parents.

One of my earliest beverage memories was at my great-grandmother's funeral in the early 1990s. I would have been about eleven; my brother David was eight. Granny had lived a happy life and finally shuffled off this mortal coil at the ripe old age of ninety-four. The service was a sombre but not altogether unjovial affair at a small-town Methodist church that smelled of mothballs and homemade strawberry jam.

My brother and I were milling around at the wake with all the other cousins, great uncles and distant family members when Aunty Mary came up to David and me, asked if we wanted a drink and handed us each a cup of orange cordial. I handed mine back and asked for a cup of tea. David screwed his nose up and asked if he could have a cappuccino. The closest thing that small-town Methodist kitchen had to an espresso machine was a screwdriver in the bottom drawer which the president of the ladies auxiliary used to prise open the commercial tin of Blend 43. Aunty Mary had no idea what a cappuccino was anyway. I think she presumed it was some sort of hat and went off to butter some scones. David wasn't impressed. I offered him some of my tea but he said it wasn't the same.

Not a whole lot has changed. Dave now owns the hippest, most award-winning café in his city. He imports his own beans from Brazil and roasts them in a factory down the road from his house. When he gets bored on weekends he runs training courses to teach wannabe baristas how to throw down a latte. If anyone was going to turn me into the ultimate hipster coffee connoisseur, he was the man.

But I didn't want to just go to a trendy city café with him, sip a few short blacks and talk about fair trade. That wasn't very ultimate. I could do that whenever I wanted. If I was going to be the biggest, bestest hipster in the land I needed to know my coffee inside out. I needed to sample a lot of it. All of it.

I called him on the phone. 'Dave,' I said. 'I'm coming to your café, we're shutting it down for the night and you're going to make me one of every coffee on the menu.'

'That's a lot of coffee,' he said. 'I didn't think you even drank coffee.'

I told him I didn't, but that this was going to be an experiment.

He said he was in.

Technically, it was possible for me to overdose on caffeine and die. According to the diagnostic criteria from the American Psychiatric Association, *Caffeine-Induced Organic Mental Disorder*, or *Caffeine Overdose*, as it was better known, was a very real and present danger.

In 2010 a British man named Michael Lee Bedford bought two teaspoons of pure caffeine powder on the internet, put them into his mouth and washed them down with an energy drink. Doctors said it was the equivalent of drinking seventy cans of Red Bull. He was dead within hours. Roughly two Americans also die each year from caffeine overdoses, but, like most Americans, they are usually massively overweight, unfit and incredibly stupid.

I was not massively overweight or unfit. On the contrary, I was fit enough to pass the Australian Army entrance physical with flying colours and my body mass index was 22.7, which is smack bang in the middle of normal. I wasn't stupid in the traditional sense, in that I had a university degree and could count to ten, but I *was* dumb enough to try and drink every coffee on a café menu.

Using a calculator and Google I figured that for my eighty-kilogram frame to terminally succumb to caffeine poisoning I would have to ingest twelve grams of the drug. The average shot of espresso had 100 mg, so if I wanted to die, I would have to drink 120 coffees. That wasn't even possible. I didn't drink 120 waters in a week. The only way I could stay awake long enough to drink 120 coffees was if I drank 120 coffees. It was ironic, but not very likely. This was good news. I probably wasn't going to die.

On the other hand, although it wasn't technically possible for me to kick the bucket, the symptoms of caffeine overdose, as described by the American Psychiatric Association, would start kicking in after a mere 250 mg of caffeine. That was just two and a half cups. If I was going to drink coffee like a proper hipster, I was going to be swallowing that for breakfast, along with a hand-rolled cigarette and a free-range bagel.

According to the professional diagnosis chart, I could expect to suffer from any number of the following symptoms:

- restlessness
- nervousness
- excitement
- insomnia
- flushed face
- diuresis
- gastrointestinal disturbance
- muscle twitching
- rambling flow of thought and speech
- tachycardia or cardiac arrhythmia
- periods of inexhaustibility
- psychomotor agitation

Given I suffered from a hundred per cent of the symptoms I'd actually *heard* of after nothing more than a weak soy latte, I was a little concerned. The symptoms I *hadn't* heard of sounded all the more alarming. As previously discussed, I was no doctor, but I knew 'cardiac' meant heart and 'arrhythmia' didn't sound pleasant; 'psychomotor agitation' even less so.

When I arrived at Dave's café after closing time I put my fears to him.

Me: Hey man, how are you?

Dave: Yeah, good. Busy day.

Me: Cool. So, I've done some research, I'd need to drink 120 coffees before it killed me. There are twenty-nine different types of coffee listed on Wikipedia. How many are on your menu?

Dave: Twelve.

Me: OK. Cool. Do you reckon I can drink twelve?

Dave: I think you can give it a red-hot go. You're not planning on sleeping tonight though, are you?

I told him I wasn't and asked what the greatest number of coffees he'd ever consumed in a day was. He said he didn't know but that it was probably somewhere around a dozen. I asked him how he felt after a dozen coffees and he said he felt 'pretty awake'.

This wasn't exactly turning out to be rocket surgery. But I wanted to know how many I could realistically expect to consume.

Me: How many coffees do you usually drink a day, though?

Dave: Two or three.

Me: OK. So you've never *tried* to drink more than twelve?

Dave: No. I'm not that stupid.

Me: Hmm.

There was an awkward pause. Dave finished typing something up in a spreadsheet and offered me half a salami sandwich. I told him I was a vegetarian for the moment and he told me I was gay.

Me: So what's the most coffees you've ever seen anyone drink?

Dave: Thirty-two.

Me: That's a lot. What happened to the person?

Dave: He was an ex-drug addict. He'd quit heroin and coffee was his new vice. There's an episode of *Futurama* or something where one of the characters drinks a hundred coffees in a day and he was trying to see if he could do it. I used to do an 'all you can drink coffee' thing and he paid for that and we got up to thirty-two before I had to cut him off.

Me: Did you count them?

Dave: Yes, I was making them for him.

Me: What happened to him after thirty-two coffees?

Dave: He had the jitters big time. He was becoming physically ill. He kept going to the toilet and said he was shitting coffee.

Me: Did he have to go to hospital?

Dave: No. He didn't drink coffee for a while after that though.

Me: Hmm.

This was concerning. Thirty-two coffees didn't sound like that much, but if a heroin addict couldn't handle it, there was no hope for me. On the other side, twelve coffees didn't sound like very much at all. That wasn't something to get excited about and put in a book. Australian cricket legend David Boon once consumed fifty-two cans of beer on a flight to London. I couldn't imagine radio stations calling up and saying: 'Hey, you're the guy who drank twelve flat whites! Come on the show!' And the internet said caffeine overdose wasn't likely to cause any long-term effects. As long as I didn't die I should be OK.

I decided to aim for sixty. Sixty coffees was half of what it would take to kill me. I'd probably get a bit shaky, but I shouldn't end up in hospital.

I asked David what he thought of that goal.

Dave: To be honest, I was being nice before when I said you could drink twelve. I think you'll be lucky to make six.

Me: Fuck you.

Dave: I know you. You're a wuss.

Me: I got a tattoo.

Dave: That's not a tattoo, that's a smudge. It looks like someone dropped a Dorito on your arm. A very small, broken Dorito.

I tried to look tough and indignant for a while. There were some coffee beans sitting on the counter so I ate a couple raw for emphasis.

Me: So, when you go to barista school, do they train you in the symptoms of caffeine overdose? What to look out for, that sort of thing?

Dave: No.

Me: I see.

Dave: If you start vomiting I'll take you to hospital though.

Me: OK thanks.

Dave: What's that? Are you knitting?

Me: Oh, yeah. It's a hipster thing.

Dave: What are you knitting?

Me: It's a scarf. For my bike.

Dave: For your what?

Me: For my bike.

Dave: You're an idiot.

Me: What's the most hipster coffee? Let's start with that.

Dave: I've been thinking about this. I'm going to make

you a double ristretto soy latte.

Me: You just made that up. You're making up words.

Dave: No I'm not. It's a thing. It's the most hipster coffee you can get. I'm going to make it for you.

Me: OK. Why's it the most hipster coffee then?

He explained that a latte was the gheyest coffee you could get because it's creamy and girly, and that hipsters like me were girly and that we had creamy skin. A soy latte was even gheyer than that because it was for vegans and vegans weren't real men.

He then explained that real men and real coffee lovers drank short black coffee. Hipsters drank coffee made from soy (and only certain brands thereof), he told me. But hipsters also valued good taste and whereas people who went to Starbucks for coffee did so because they liked the taste of milk, proper hipster coffee lovers liked the taste of *coffee*, so that's why they went to the trouble of ordering things like a double ristretto.

I asked him what a ristretto was. He explained that when you pour a shot of espresso from a coffee machine, the first part that pours out is the fatty acids from the beans which form a crema on top. As the coffee keeps pouring the crema turns into basically muddy water. If you only pour the first half of the shot you just get the sweet crema bit and that, on its own, is a ristretto. If you pour two ristrettos you end up with the same amount of coffee as a normal shot, but you only get the best part.

It made sense.

Me: Why don't you just make it like that all the time then?

Dave: A full shot has its merits. There's more acidity. More citrus flavours.

Me: You mean it's bitter.

Dave: We tend not to use the word 'bitter'.

Me: You're a wanker.

Dave: Do you want one or not?

Me: Yes.

So he made me coffee number one—a soy latte double ristretto. It was nice. Creamy. Like he said. I sipped it. Then I noticed he wasn't having one. I asked him why he wasn't having one. He said he'd already had three today, that that would do him and that he didn't want to OD on caffeine because someone had to stay sane to drive me to the hospital. I said fair enough.

I finished the coffee and put the glass down on the counter.

Dave: How are you feeling?

Me: Good. Awake. A little shaky already, but I'm OK. What's next?

Dave: Soy macchiato.

Me: Bring it on.

A soy macchiato was apparently the second most hipster coffee in the world. This was because a proper macchiato was literally only a shot of espresso coffee which had been stained by a very small amount of milk—nothing more than a teaspoon of froth on top. You would only ever ask for a soy macchiato if you were a complete wanker, my brother told me, because you'd have to be some sort of wine-tasting professional, or a perfume maker, or some sort of bomb sniffer dog to be able to tell the difference between a millilitre of soy milk foam and a millilitre of real milk foam when it was sitting on a shot of espresso. And even if you could, it would be pointless, because the amount of milk used was so small it was probably going to go to waste anyway, so it wasn't like you were hurting any extra cows. Even though they liked getting milked anyway.

I asked for two soy macchiatos. They appeared. I drank them and he made me a salad sandwich.

'Eat that or you're going to get sick,' he said.

I obliged. We let the sandwich settle in and he asked me how I was feeling. The truth was, I was feeling OK. It was good coffee and he was a good barista, so the effects weren't too bad. There was a definite caffeine buzz starting to set in, but nothing too serious just yet.

Dave: OK. You ready for dessert?

Me: Shouldn't we drink some more coffee?

Dave: Yes, I'm going to make you coffee dessert, you idiot.

I said I was in.

He made an iced coffee first up. That was good. It had ice cream in it and I asked for chocolate topping, which he said wasn't very hipster, but he'd let it slide. That went down pretty easily so he whipped up an Irish coffee with Baileys in it. I liked that too. This wasn't hard at all. I was already five shots in and feeling fine. It felt like I was cheating a little though, disguising the coffee with other delicious masking agents, so we decided to go a little more hardcore and I had two short blacks in quick succession, like shots of tequila. I decided to shoot them back with a lick of sugar and a suck of chocolate too. He thought that was pretty funny.

That's about the point I started hiccupping.

My hiccups are famous. They sound like someone is torturing a small, yet surprisingly vocal frog to death with a nine iron. David thought they were funny and said the best way to cure the hiccups was drinking a long black upside down. He made a long black for me and put some ice in it to cool it down a bit.

I can't stand on my head by myself so he put the glass on the ground with a straw next to my face and held my feet up in the air while I drank it quickly. This made me choke and coffee went everywhere. He dropped my legs and I fell over, taking the coffee with me.

Dave said that since I'd spilt almost all of the long black he couldn't count it in the tally. I tried to protest but could only hiccup in response. He rubbed the day's special off the little blackboard menu and made seven marks on it instead.

'Seven,' he said. 'You're up to seven. That's pretty good. I thought you were only going to make five, to be honest.'

I told him to fuck off and make me an affogato. I knew about affogatos. They were coffee with ice cream in them. Like an ice cream sundae. I wanted one. I went to the toilet, twice, and he made me one. We let that settle and I eventually stopped hiccupping.

'How are you feeling now?' he asked, and put another mark on the blackboard.

I thought about it. I was tapping my foot wildly.

'I feel dizzy,' I said. 'And I don't want to go upside down again.'

He nodded.

'And my flushed is face and I'm having trouble concentrating on what I'm saying.'

He nodded again. I think that part was becoming obvious.

'But we're up to eight and I want to go for sixty.'

He said OK, but that sixty was a long way from eight. He asked me how many sixty was from eight. I said it was fifty-two, the same number as David Boon drank on the plane.

'OK, your maths is still good enough,' Dave said. 'You're clearly not dying. So let's make you a hipster triple—a soy latte, a soy flat white and a soyccino. Then, if you can even get those down, I think you're going to be too full and we're going to have to go back to shots.'

I said OK.

He brought three drinks out and explained the difference between a flat white and a latte. I'm sure he did a brilliant job of it, but by that point I was starting to find it incredibly hard to concentrate. I had also started going to the bathroom a lot. It was like someone had given me ten beers, five Valiums and a shot of amphetamines. Intravenously. Into my eyeballs.

I managed to finish the latte and the flat white and I think I even managed to convince Dave I understood the difference between them, but when I started rocking backwards and forwards I'm fairly certain he started to realise something was wrong.

'Dude, are you sure you're OK?' he asked. 'You look pale. Really pale. And you're rocking.'

'How many shots have I had now?' I asked.

'Well, you've had ten all up, not counting the long black you choked on, and you're halfway through the cino, so, ten and a half.'

I finished the soy cino and held up all my fingers.

'Well, that's ten, but I think you mean eleven.'

I told him I was going to the bathroom again. He said he thought that would be a good idea.

I went to the bathroom and had to sit down. The room was spinning. I didn't even bother wiping the seat or carefully placing toilet paper down so my bottom didn't touch anything. My heart was racing and I could feel myself breathing heavily. This wasn't good at all. I pulled out my iPhone and started to Google 'psychomotor agitation'—I realised I'd forgotten to do that earlier and I still didn't know what it was—but I was shaking too much to type properly. I was also incredibly thirsty, which didn't make any sense at all, given I'd had eleven cups of liquid in a couple of hours. I went to the sink and drank like a puppy for about thirty seconds. That made me feel a little better so I went back out to the café.

Dave looked worried.

'Are you OK? Did you vom-vom?' he asked.

'I didn't puke, but no, no I'm not feeling too well,' I said.

He told me to sit down. I sat down.

'Have I had everything on the menu?' I asked.

He said I hadn't. I swore.

'What do I do?'

He shrugged. 'Why don't you sit down for a while and chill out?'

That seemed like a good idea. We waited for ten minutes and I tried to explain how to knit but my fingers felt too weak and shaky to hold the needles. God knows how nannas with arthritis did it. I got him to explain what fair trade was instead. It was something about buying lots of coffee from Ethiopians and apparently it wasn't very fair at all.

'What else is on the menu?' I asked.

'Well, let me see. You haven't had a Café Bombón, a mocha or a Vienna coffee yet. And that's not counting all the milk versions of everything; you've only had soy milk so far.'

I said that was OK because hipsters only drank soy milk.

'Do you think you can drink any more?' he asked.

I told him I was going to drink forty-eight more and threw a knitting needle at him. It missed. By quite a long way. He said he didn't think it would be a good idea if I had any more coffee. I said it was a brilliant idea and that if he refused I was going to find the nearest 24-hour McCafé and start drinking there. That shut him up. He said he would rather I died than went to a McCafé. I agreed.

'Make me a Vienna café mocha Bombón then,' I said. 'Just put it all in the one mug.'

'They go in a glass,' he said.

'Even better.'

He told me that a Café Bombón was made with sweetened condensed milk, a mocha was made with cocoa and that a Vienna was made with cream. If he put them all into the one glass with three shots of espresso it would be so rich I would almost certainly spew. I said I felt fine and to just do it.

He did. I drank it. I spewed. It was only a little spew, about two shots worth, but it was definitely a spew.

He said he told me so and rubbed a couple of marks off the board.

I fell over.

'I'm driving you home,' he told me. I said OK and asked what the tally was. He said I'd had fourteen shots and spewed about two—which left twelve. I took a photo of the blackboard for proof. It wasn't a record-breaking innings by any means, but at least I had learned what a soy latte double ristretto was. And that was pretty hip.

I'd planned a trip to a bunch of trendy cafés the next morning to put my theory into practice, followed by some hipster bars to get hipfaced. All I had to do now was get some sleep.

CHAPTER 17
I DIAL 000 BECAUSE SOMEONE IS BEING MURDERED IN MY BACKYARD

Most people go through life not knowing the precise number of louvres on every venetian blind in their entire house. Fewer still decide to solve the puzzle at two am. Thanks to my new friend, caffeine, a whole world of opportunities had arisen. Some people clean things when they're having a bit of a coffee buzz. Others exercise. I had decided to count. It started with sheep.

My brother had dropped me home from his café at about ten pm and I'd showered, cleaned my teeth three times, re-laced every pair of shoes I owned and had a private skipping contest with the cat before turning in. I say 'turning in' because I went to bed and then turned and tossed for three hours before realising I would not be sleeping for a long time. Possibly not till Christmas.

My dad always used to tell me as a kid that the best way to fall asleep was to try and think nothing. If you can think nothing after twelve cups of coffee you are either dead or a Justin Bieber fan. So I counted sheep instead. All of them. There are forty million sheep in New Zealand and one hundred and twenty million sheep in Australia and I tallied every single one. When I ran out of sheep, I started counting pigs, but I could only remember four —

the three little ones and Babe—so I moved on to venetian-blind louvres.

The problem with counting louvres is that you can't blink or you lose track of where you're at. Ordinarily this would be something of an issue, but after twelve cups of coffee, I was only blinking once every hour. This made it exceptionally easy to count louvres, but it also gave me a blinding headache.

Hipsters don't have a whole lot of vices. Alcohol and coffee are the obvious ones. They'll throw down a bunch of pills at a music festival if there's something dancey on, and they're certainly not worried about inhaling if someone passes around a joint at a party, but of all the drugs in the world hipsters are known for taking, it's the legal ones which are the most notorious. The cool kids are all on something. The Queens of the Stone Age indie anthem (and festival pharmaceutical field guide) 'Feel Good Hit of the Summer' sums it up perfectly in one chorus: 'nicotine, Valium, Vicodin, marijuana, ecstasy and alcohol'. Two of those are illegal, four are not (depending on your relationship with the local medical centre). I rest my case.

I'd never been a user or abuser of prescription drugs, but after twelve coffees, 392 louvres and no sleep I had a headache which required serious amateur medical attention.

Luckily I had been quite sick a few months before. Not man-flu sick: proper sick. I had been in a lot of pain and after three days of not being able to eat or sleep because of the hand grenade gently exploding in my stomach, I had decided to go to the doctor. She told me I should have gone to the emergency ward three days earlier but that if I'd come this far I probably wasn't going to get any worse. In case the grenade turned into an atom bomb and my pancreas literally exploded, she gave me a note saying that if I turned up at an emergency ward they had to let me in and give me head pats and sympathetic looks and their very best stethoscope.

As far as important pieces of paper go, a note from a doctor is out-ranked only by a diplomatic passport. You can get out of a parking ticket with a note from your doctor. You can get out of wearing a helmet on a motorbike. You can get out of the Commonwealth Games. You can use one to get a disabled parking permit. Should you and thirty-two colleagues ever happen to find yourself stuck down a South American mine, a note from your doctor will even get you cigarettes.

I didn't end up needing the note from my doctor to get me into hospital (luckily) but I did have one of those other fabulous doctor notes up my sleeve. One of the ones that gets you pain medication. The prescription said I could have pretty much whatever drugs I wanted from a chemist of my choosing. I have drawn a table to illustrate where, in the scheme of pharmaceuticals, the ones I ended up with slotted in, in terms of potency:

1. The vial of morphine they give the dashing young private when he's been shot up real bad in every war film ever made. Not the first vial to ease the pain, the one *after* he keeps sobbing for Ma and the medic knows he's going to die because his insides are outside and they have to put

him out of his misery and the medic looks at the sarge
and the sarge nods and the medic nods back and then
rips a package open with his teeth and sticks a vial in his
leg; those drugs.

2. The drugs that killed River Phoenix
3. **My drugs**
4. Whatever Joaquin Phoenix has been on
5. Crack cocaine
6. Crystal meth
7. Whatever you can scrape up off the steps of the Opera
   House after the ARIAs
8. Magic mushrooms
9. Medicinal marijuana
10. Panadol

My drugs, I swear, contained sixty per cent medicinal LSD
and sixty per cent hydroponic heroin. You could have
performed tusk canal surgery on an elephant after one of
them. My doctor had prescribed me two every four hours
and said not to be shy with them.

I had taken a few at the time and they'd worked wonders.
If they could ease stomach pain, surely they'd snuff my
headache out as well. While I was at it, I figured I might
as well knock back a couple more to help me sleep. And
throw in a Valium for good measure.

I took four pain drugs and a Valium and waited for Alice
to throw a grenade down the rabbit hole and take me
along for the ride. Sadly, she didn't turn up, but at four
am, someone—or something—else did. In my caffeinated
delirium I began hearing a god-awful, gutteral, groaning

noise in my backyard. It sounded to me like someone had been stabbed repeatedly and left for dead under my bedroom window.

On any normal Friday evening I would have put on some pants and lights and gone to investigate, but I was still offhandedly convulsing from the coffee and too confused to even find the light, let alone fend off marauding murderers.

I live across the road from a mental hospital which mostly treats people with eating disorders, but I'd checked their website a few days earlier and noticed they also cared for 'psycho-geriatrics'. My hipster apartment, being on the edge of the funky creative part of town, was also a brisk ten- to fifteen-minute stumble from the loitering-places of ninety per cent of the city's homeless drug addicts. They never tended to wander as far as my place, but judging by the sound coming from outside, some crazed old Vietnam vet appeared to have broken out of his straightjacket, got on the bourbon and lured a few stragglers down our way for some casual smiting.

After a couple of minutes the groaning began to get louder and, fearing seriously for my life and high on a hipster party mix of caffeine, codeine and benzodiazepine, I decided to dial 000 and ask for the police. The conversation went pretty much like this . . .

Me: Hello?

Policeman: Yes, hello, what assistance do you need?

Me: Well, I think, there's like a groaning sound. In the backyard. Sort of a moaning and groaning.

Policeman: What's your address there?

Me: Unit 3, 248 New Farm Drive.

Policeman: (taking notes) Unit 3, 248 New Farm Drive.

Me: No, wait. 284. I only just moved in a bit over a year ago and I forget sometimes.

Policeman: You 'only just' moved in a bit over a year ago?

Me: Yeah, I forget sometimes.

Policeman: OK. And what's your phone number there?

Me: Oh, I thought you would have had it because of caller ID.

Policeman: Can you just confirm it for me please?

Me: Umm, yep. It's 04 . . .

Policeman: OK, and what's the problem?

Me: Well (whispering) I'm whispering so they can't hear. There's like, hang on, I'll move away from the window. There's like a moaning. Sort of a moaning. Groaning. It sounds like someone is dying. Umm. It's a really weird sound. Sort of like 'aargh, eeergh, aargh'.

Policeman: Right.

Me: Kind of an 'eergh, eerga argh'.

Policeman: And how long have you been hearing the noise?

Me: It's been going for about five minutes now. It's really in-human.

Policeman: Sorry, did you say it was human or in-human?

Me: No. Well, yeah. Sort of non-human. But I'm sure it's human. It's like the weirdest human sound ever. It kind of sounds like an animal, but coming from a human. I studied music technology at uni so I know about frequencies and things and it's definitely a person. Definitely. Almost certainly. I think someone has been stabbed or something.

Policeman: So, where is the person in relation to you?

Me: It's out the back. Near my bedroom window.

Policeman: Can you see the person?

Me: No. It's really dark. I think they're near the tree.

Policeman: Near the tree?

Me: I think so. Kind of, I think they're in the tree now.

Policeman: In the tree.

Me: Yep. They were on the ground before, but I think they're in the tree now.

Policeman: Did you hear an altercation?

Me: No, I was lying in bed and I just started hearing this 'eerk argh'. It was really loud . . . Wait. There it goes again. Can you hear it? It's really loud. I'll hold the phone up.

Policeman: OK.

Me: Did you hear it?

Policeman: I don't think so.

Me: Really? It's really loud. It's like an 'ach, argh argh'.

Policeman: OK.

Me: Hang on, I think it's wandering off.

Policeman: Has it stopped?

Me: No, it's just wandering off. It's kind of chanting now.

Policeman: Chatting?

Me: Chanting. Kind of 'acheyah, ooyah, acheyah'.

Policeman: OK.

Me: It's just that I live near a mental hospital and there's lots of drug addicts in the Valley and I thought maybe one of them had been (whispering) killed.

Police: And so you can just hear the one, ah, person at present?

Me: Oh, it's kind of getting higher. Near the tree out the back. It's kind of shrieking now.

Policeman: Is it in the tree?

Me: I can't see it. I'm too scared to turn the light on. I had a lot of coffee, a LOT of coffee and I had to sit down to pee before because I thought I was going to faint so I'm a bit weak and I'm on some really heavy dru— Nothing. I'm fine.

Policeman: Sorry, what did you say you were on? Are you sure you're OK?

Me: No, I'm a bit sick, but I think it's moving away.

Policeman: In the tree?

Me: Yes. Maybe. No. Maybe. Yes. In the tree. I'm not sure.

Policeman: It's not a possum, is it?

Me: Yeah. Could be.

CHAPTER 18
HIPSTERDRUNK

So it was time to get drunk in the name of science. Einstein would have used that excuse a lot, I'm sure. There must have been times when he didn't want to go give a lecture or save the world, so I'm certain he would have had some sort of shed out the back where he could listen to the football, sink lager and hide from government officials who came pleading for assistance beating the Germans. Sure, one or two of the smarter CIA types probably managed to get past Mrs Einstein and sneak around the side gate, but he would have had a bevy of excuses at hand.

'Albert mate, there's been a bit of an issue over at the nuclear lab, some atoms have gone missing and blown up a fair portion of Nevada, are you right to pop down and help us out for a tick?'

'Fuck, love to mate, but I can't.' He'd hold up a longneck. 'Doing some research. Bubbles. It's complex. Can't leave the couch.'

The government official would have no comeback for that. When you discover the theory of relativity you can get away with that sort of thing. Isaac Newtown was the same. Used to get on the cider a bit if he knew there was a grade five science class coming around to hear about gravity.

I, on the other hand, didn't often get to use the science excuse. In fact, I dropped out of biology in grade ten, so it was rare for me to be able to drink in the name of the greater good of humanity. Usually it was to the detriment of humanity. Perhaps not all of humanity. Certainly a handful of representatives though, depending on the level of intoxication. It's not that I'm a violent drunk—on the contrary, I just get happy and chatty, then I climb things, then I fall asleep and snore like there's a freight train trying to escape my nose. I once kept an entire Italian backpacker hostel awake for a night when I fell asleep in the doorway after drinking three bottles of homemade sambucca with the owner and then snored so loudly they thought a lion had escaped the colosseum and was being beaten to death on the street outside with a foghorn. The next day I vomited in the Sistine Chapel. I'm still not allowed back in the Vatican. If I do make it to heaven they're going to put me on toilet-cleaning duty for two eternities to make up for it.

But penance could wait. I was at the pointy end of ultimate hipsterdom. It was time to put the lattes down and hit the hard stuff. I was ready. I was born ready. I'd been in rock and roll bands since I was sixteen and I had trained for this moment. The only problem I had was knowing exactly which hard stuff to hit.

Alcohol stays within tribal boundaries. Pick a border—any border, anywhere in the world. It doesn't have to be a national border: pick a state border. Pick a right side of the tracks and a wrong side of the tracks and either side will have a different favourite drink. A beer hated in one city will be adored twenty miles down the road. Wines are defined by their regions. Whiskey varies in spelling and ingredients depending on the continent, and the incontinent for that matter. Depending on which city you're in, your martini either has vodka or gin. The only constants are tequila, which is drunk exclusively by Mexicans and teenagers on spring break, and rum, which is only consumed by pirates and racist, homophobic, wife-beating fuckwits.

In America the unanimous hipster drink of choice is Pabst Blue Ribbon. It's so typically hipster it has become a stereotype. The strange thing is that Pabst isn't so much a blue-ribbon beer as it is a blue-collar beer. It's cheap, easy to drink and everywhere. To the outsider it probably seems like a strange choice for a generation of children priding themselves on organic, boutique, alternative everything else. Nevertheless, it wasn't my problem—there is no way to get Pabst in Australia. And believe me I've tried. Nobody can order it in. Even specialist American food importers can't get it. No bottle shop in Australia stocks Pabst. The reason seems to be because it is completely shithouse. I even went so far as offering friends travelling in America handsome sums of money to secure me JUST ONE bottle, but the resounding response was always an unequivocal, 'Mate, you don't want it, trust me'.

So I'd resigned myself to not becoming a Pabst Blue Ribbon drinker on my quest, but no matter. There were other beverages to choose from. And hipsters didn't only live in America. There were just as many in London and Sydney as there were in Brooklyn. There was literally a world of other beverages to choose from.

You could argue that since the zero meridian, where Greenwich Mean Time begins, is in East London, East

London hipsters should literally be the first to know what's cool. Since I wasn't going to be getting any Pabst, I figured I might as well turn to an East Ender for advice. Luckily I already had one planted in the field doing recon. When Chris, the singer from my old band, had moved to London a year before, he landed himself in the heart of Shoreditch—hipster capital of Europe, if not the world. He was an oracle of London hipster advice, at least on most occasions.

I didn't know what time it would be when I wanted the answer to my question, so I sent him a text message. I don't know if he was drunk, but he did seem to struggle a little with the answer:

Me: Hey mate, what do all the cool kids in London drink?

Chris: The most hip area is easy London, where I live :) more specifically the clubs in Shoreditch, and I just heard the 'cat and mutton' is the most hipster pub in London. It's awesome, right on Broadway Market which French Vogue recently named the coolest or 'most hip' place on earth :) my local

Me: Awesome, we shall go there, but I was more interested in WHAT they drank, notsomuch where

Chris: East London sorry

Me: So I was looking for an answer along the lines of 'beer', or perhaps 'cider', and then maybe a particular brand. So, for example, Heineken is a brand of beer, and Bulmers is a brand of cider. Something like that.

Chris: Oh, sorry. Red Stripe. It's a beer.

This was useful information. I did some Googling and discovered I could get Red Stripe beer in Australia. Tick.

Next I had to figure out what was the most hipster Australian beverage. That turned out to be harder than I thought.

To my knowledge, and I was by now pretty much the ultimate hipster so my head was full of hipster knowledge, the hippest beverage in this country was pear cider. Almost all the cool kids I knew drank it. I drank it. I liked it. All the hipster bars sold it. Beer is so mainstream; it stood to reason that cider, and not just any cider, but its more alternate version *pear* cider, would fill the kegs of hipsterland.

I was all set to go on a pear cider tasting mission when I made the mistake of putting the call out to everyone I knew asking what they thought the ultimate hipster drink was. Predictably, the answers were wild and varied.

A friend whose job was programming *rage*, possibly the most hipster television show in the country save for ironic re-runs of *MacGyver*, said she was, like, so over pear cider and had moved on to ginger beer. That idea was confirmed by another photographer friend who was adamant that Crabbie's Ginger Beer, an English brand, was the ultimate alt brew.

I was beginning to think I was behind the times, but then another friend whose job was reviewing movies for the same hipster radio station as Hipster Radio Station Ex-Girlfriend, agreed with me and said pear cider was definitely the most hipster drink in the country.

Another mate who worked in a bank and liked the Dave Matthews Band, which should have made his opinion roughly as relevant as my mother's, threw a curveball and said Melbourne Bitter longnecks were what the cool crowd was drinking down south. The idea actually had merit. Melbourne Bitter is to this country what Pabst is to New Yorkers. I was actually thinking of starting an ironic hipster VB revolution myself. Melbourne Bitter was one better.

Then, not to be outdone, the humble grape found itself represented by two very distinct, very opposite points of view. Cask wine is all baby hipsters can afford and all my hip university friends went to great lengths to convince me that it was at the number one drink of choice for anyone who was anyone. All my older, wiser, hipper friends were horrified at the thought and were resolute that a bottle of red wine in a park, drunk alone while reading a good book was as cool as it was possible to get. I'm sure Ernest Hemingway would have agreed.

Faced with a choice between a pear cider, a wine, a beer or a ginger beer tasting session, I decided the only way to scientifically prove which drink was the most hipster would be to drink copious amounts of all of them.

I would need support for this. Moral support for one, and probably physical support as well—I would have to stand up and find my way home at some stage—so I called up Jodie. I hadn't seen her since we'd hung out and she'd promised me that if I ever needed help with my quest, she'd be happy to get on board. It was early on a Sunday morning so I didn't imagine she'd be awake, but I figured I'd leave a message and get her to call me back as soon as she could and we'd make a plan. Strangely enough, she answered . . .

Jodie: Hello?

Me: Oh hey, it's Matt, what the hell are you doing up—
it's seven am?

Jodie: I haven't been to bed. What are you doing up?

Me: I had a few coffees last night. Couldn't sleep.

Jodie: Oh great! Well done. I'm impressed. How many
did you have?

Me: Twelve.

Jodie: Twelve what?

Me: Coffees.

Jodie: You had twelve coffees?

Me: Yeah, and then I couldn't sleep.

Jodie: I'm not surprised.

Me: Hey, what are you doing today?

Jodie: Why?

Me: We need to get drunk in the name of science.

Jodie: What, now?

Me: (looking at my watch) Yeah.

Jodie: (thinks for one or two seconds) OK. I'm actually in
Sydney at the moment, but my flight leaves in an hour. I'll
come and meet you.

'Is that a scarf on your bike?' Jodie asked. I'd taken the train
to meet her at the airport and I'd brought Trixie with me.

I told her it was.

She nodded. 'Why is there a scarf on your bike?'

'Because I bought too much yarn and I didn't know what

else to do with it, so I figured I'd make a scarf to cover my bike,' I said. 'It also stops it getting scratched when I play bike polo. Cool, huh?'

'Why are you carrying a bag of tomatoes?' she asked.

'These are heirloom tomatoes,' I explained. I'd finally found some. 'I picked them up from a market stall on the way here. They're really hard to get. I'm going to give you one. You should be glad.'

She had a look. She couldn't understand why they were hard to get. They looked like they'd fallen off the back of a truck. They probably had fallen off the back of a truck. I didn't mind though. I was happy. Another box ticked.

'Hey, what did you do last night?' I asked, curious as to why she was still awake and in Sydney at seven am on a Sunday. It was impressively late even for a thirty-year-old vegan hipster. I didn't think she'd have enough energy to last that long.

'I don't remember. But it started out in Kings Cross and then there was some cider and then some more cider and then you rang and here I am.'

'Cool,' I said. 'Did you have trouble getting a flight?'

'No, I was about to go to bed when you called but I was already dressed so I just went straight to the airport and there was one leaving. Also, I have $2000 in Monopoly money in my pocket. It's all in $20 notes. I don't know where it came from.'

This was an interesting and unexpected piece of information.

'Did you sell Monopoly drugs to someone?' I asked. One of the airport security staff thought he overheard something. He motioned for me to take my bicycle outside.

'No,' Jodie said. 'Don't say that so loud.'

'Sorry. That's weird,' I said. 'Weird but good. I was going to suggest we take the train back to my place, but I think we should take a top hat and a battleship instead.'

'In this condition I'm going to need a wheelbarrow. Anyway, explain what we're doing. Why are we drinking in the name of science?'

I explained we had to determine what the ultimate hipster beverage was.

'OK, and what are the candidates?'

'Pear cider,' I said. She nodded. 'And Red Stripe beer: it's from the UK.' She nodded again. 'And cask wine. And nice red wine. And ginger beer.'

'Is that all?' Jodie asked, with perhaps a hint of sarcasm.

'And Melbourne Bitter longnecks.'

'I see.'

Jodie said she was starting to feel a bit hungover. I asked her if she was going to vomit. She said maybe. She asked if we had to drink Melbourne Bitter longnecks. I explained that she could opt for VB if she wanted, but that I would be drinking Melbourne Bitter longnecks. Two of them. Minimum. And that she would be joining me.

'OK,' she said. 'What are we starting with?'

I hadn't thought about this.

'What time is it in London?' I asked.

'I don't know,' she said. 'One-thirty am maybe?'

'OK cool, let me make a phone call.'

I dialled Chris in London and asked him where he was. He was at a party. I asked him if anyone was drinking

Red Stripe beer. He looked around and reported that most of the people at the party were drinking Red Stripe beer. Someone was drinking cider. Somebody else was trying, unsuccessfully, to climb the refrigerator. I asked him if the people drinking Red Stripe beer looked cool. He said they looked cool. I thanked him and hung up.

'We're starting with Red Stripe beer,' I told Jodie.

'OK, do you have any?'

'No.'

So we set about finding some Red Stripe beer.

'Red Back beer?' was the most common response we got. 'No,' we'd reply. 'Red Stripe beer. It's from London.' We went to five bottle shops before anyone had any idea what we were talking about. Finally a little boutique place had some clue. 'Ah, from Jamaica?' said the woman behind the counter. She was English.

'No, it's English,' I replied.

'No. It's Jamaican. Mon. They just drink it in London. And there's a six-pack over there.' She pointed to a corner of the fridge over to the side and down the bottom near some weird non-Corona Mexican brew. It was $25, which seemed steep, but I wasn't about to put a price on ultimate hipsterdom.

She also had Crabbie's Ginger Beer, which was another item ticked off the shopping list. I grabbed some pinot noir and some Melbourne Bitter longnecks from her too. The only thing she didn't have was cask wine. I had to go back to a larger chain bottle shop for that. Jodie protested but I said she had to man up in the name of science.

'What about pear cider?' she asked. 'Isn't that the main event? You haven't bought any pear cider.'

I told her we were going to a bar for that. A bar that sold nine different kinds of pear cider. She liked this idea. We did a stocktake. We had all the alcohol.

'Where are we drinking the rest of the ultimate hipster booze then?' she asked.

'Dude,' I said. 'The ultimate hipster park.'

'We're going to New York?'

'Did you bring your passport?' I asked.

She patted herself down. 'No. You didn't tell me we were going to New York.'

'We'll go to New York next time,' I said. 'Until then, New Farm Park will do. It's tindie-as anyway.'

'Did you just say tindie?'

'Oh, it means touch of indie,' I said.

'I don't know you.'

We grabbed some fake Ray-Bans left over from my market stall and a picnic blanket from my house. Jodie's eyes weren't in outdoor condition and her pants were new. She didn't want to stain a $300 pair of boating slacks on the grass. The picnic blanket had a pattern on it similar to flannelette so I called it the hipnic blanket. She suggested we get a game of Scrabble to pass the time, but I explained Scrabble pieces were hard to come by and I only had one letter and it was on a ring, so it wasn't much good. We had our phones though: we could play each other on them.

Snacks were also a necessity. We picked up some hommus, crackers, olives, organic sourdough bread and organic goat's cheese to go with the heirloom tomatoes. Jodie said I could get some prosciutto as well if I wanted. I said OK. She called me a murderer.

This prompted a lengthy discussion about sustainability in which she called me a fascist and I referred to her as a tree-hugging hippie fuckwit. We decided to agree to disagree and by that time we were at the park, so we fought over who got to sit on the Esky instead. I won the argument and took the first shift while she lay down on the hipnic blanket. It was by now midday so the park was starting to fill up with picnicking families and hipnicking tindie kids.

We sat down, looked at the clear sky, looked at the green grass, and despite our respective hangovers and complete lack of sleep, we smiled. It was a beautiful day. If it had been 1934 our smiles would have been described by Enid Blyton as 'gay'.

After a moment of silence to admire our surroundings, I handed her a Red Stripe.

'So, explain to me why this is cool?' she said.

I revealed that all the cool kids in London drank Red Stripe, and that they were closest to the international dateline, so they knew what was cool first.

'Dude, the international dateline is in the Pacific Ocean. Near Samoa.'

'No,' I said. 'It's in London. At Greenwich. There's a line, I've stood on it. There's a boat there.'

'No,' she said. 'That's the zero degrees line. That's just where they start counting how far it is around the world.'

I thought about this for a second.

'Well then that means East London hipsters are closest to the start of the world, so either way, my argument is valid.'

She thought this had merit.

We took a sip.

'We can get some Samoan beer too if you like,' I offered.

'Do they even have beer in Samoa?' she asked.

I told her it was hot, so of course they had beer.

We decided that Red Stripe beer tasted like goat's piss. Jodie suggested we have another one to be sure. I decided that since we were drinking in the name of science we should really decide what Red Stripe beer tasted like based on a sample of three and introduce a control beer to be sure.

After three Red Stripes and a longneck of Melbourne Bitter we came to the conclusion that Red Stripe tasted like beer and that Melbourne Bitter tasted like goat's piss. I wrote this down in my Moleskine notebook in a table I'd headed 'tasting notes'. There was another column next to the tasting notes which was titled 'tick here if this is the ultimate hipster beverage'. I left that column blank. We had a way to go yet.

'How are you feeling?' Jodie asked me.

I looked around to take in my bearings and glanced at my watch. We'd been there for an hour and a half already.

'Drunk,' I said. I looked at my watch again. I had a habit of looking at my watch and then forgetting the time immediately after. I'd been up for thirty hours straight. 'Sort of drunk and hungover both at the same time. And tired.'

'Do you want a coffee?'

I said I didn't want a coffee.

I brought out another longneck. 'Let's have this,' I said. 'This will take away some of the hangover feeling.'

We agreed that Melbourne Bitter still tasted like goat's piss, but that it was better than the cask wine was going to be, so we should get a little drunker before we started on that.

'So you're still on a quest to be the ultimate hipster, right?' Jodie asked.

I said that nothing had changed

'How will you know when you've reached the end?'

I hadn't thought about this.

'What if you already are the ultimate hipster? In fact, Matt, look at you. Look at your tattoo, your sunglasses, everything. You're drinking a longneck in the park on a Sunday. You're an administrator for a disused online amateur fashion photography community. You have a Korean grunge band; you have a fucking homemade scarf for your fixed-gear vegetarian bicycle. I'm going to repeat that for emphasis. You have a scarf on your bicycle. What if this is as hip as it gets?'

I said nothing. I hadn't thought about this at all. What if she was right? 'Wait a minute. Are you just saying that to get out of drinking goon?'

'Little bit.'

'Fuck you.'

I got a wine glass out of the Esky and poured us each a large lashing of Lambrusco from the cask.

'I was kidding,' she said. 'But seriously, though, how will you know when you're the ultimate hipster? It's not like you're going to get some award or anything. There are no hipster Olympics you can win. When are you going to stop?'

'I can't stop yet,' I said. 'We haven't had any pear cider.'

Jodie said it was a fair point. 'Yeah, OK. And then?'

I thought about it some more.

'Well, to be honest, I don't know. I'm a little bit lacking in the ultimate hipster girlfriend stakes that's for sure.'

She nodded.

We had a look around.

'I can't see any ultimate hipster girlfriends here,' Jodie said.

'No, there's none here. I already checked. I thought I saw one a while ago, though.'

'What happened?' she asked.

'She tried to get my phone number for her friend.'

'That's not a bad thing.'

'Her friend was a man.'

'Ah.' Jodie nodded. 'Were you knitting a scarf at the time?'

'Little bit.'

She patted me on the back. 'I'll give you a hot tip.'

'Shut up.'

I poured us each another glass of Lambrusco.

'What do you think of the goon?' I asked.

'It tastes like university,' she said.

We sculled it.

'So you know where you might have a better chance of finding the ultimate hipster girlfriend?' Jodie asked.

'Where?'

'In a bar.'

I said she had a good point.

'So why don't we stop drinking shit goon in the park and go to a bar?'

I said we had to finish the good wine first because I wasn't carrying the bottle back home and to be the ultimate hipster I had to drink good wine in a park before dark.

So we did. We finished the wine. And the ginger beer. And a fair portion of the cask wine. I beat Jodie at Scrabble. She beat me at Scrabble.

We played chess on our phones. We went to music blogs on our phones and downloaded songs we'd never heard of to play loudly in the park through the little phone speakers. A woman came up to us to ask for directions. A dog wandered by and tried to steal our prosciutto. I forgot I was a vegetarian and ate it instead. Jodie reminded me I was supposed to be a vegetarian and I tried to get her to do the Heimlich manoeuvre so I would throw it back up again. I couldn't. Some kids lost their tennis ball close to us and we played soccer with it before kicking it back. We fell over. Their parents didn't like us. The kids had to go play in another part of the park.

We looked for four-leaf clovers and found a five-leaf clover. We missed the bus. We missed the next bus. We decided to walk. We walked. We made it home. We wanted a nap. I had a coffee. I had another coffee. I almost vomited. Jodie had a coffee. Jodie vomited. We sat on the couch and stared. How drunk are you? How drunk are *you*? Music blared. We decided to go out. We decided not to go out. It was eight pm.

We had to go out. There was science at stake.

And I'd completely forgotten to arrange a venue for TRI△NGLR's first gig. It was now or never.

I called a taxi and got us a couple of scarves. The wind was picking up.

CHAPTER 19
HIP AND RUN

It was still relatively early by the time we got to the hippest bar in the city, and it was a Sunday night, but it was already packed with cool kids, including a group of about twenty deaf people who were chatting to each other using sign language. It was strange watching them because the rest of their body language wasn't any different from anyone else's, they were wearing the same clothes, they had the same drinks and the same laughter, but they were completely silent. It was eerie. They were having some sort of party and they were hogging most of the couches, leaving only a few spare seats here and there. I wanted to chat to someone about getting a gig so I told Jodie to go and steal a spot with the deaf people while I chatted.

She insisted that since she used to be a model and had run fashion shows, her gig negotiation skills were on par with, if not better than, mine, and that she would help out—a point she emphasised by slamming her hand down on the bar and knocking over a number of empty glasses. This got the bartender's attention. I didn't want to start an argument in front of the staff, so I smiled and started up a conversation.

'So, what's the most hipster drink you sell?' I asked, keen for some professional input.

The bartender looked confused.

'What do you mean by hipster?' he asked. The music was loud, so he almost had to shout.

'Tindie.' I said.

'Tindie?'

I looked around the room. 'Like, you know, what's popular here?'

'You want a beer?'

I shook my head. 'No, no, what's popular *here*.' I pointed at the bar in front of me to indicate where I meant. He looked down. The bar was draped with a long barmat emblazoned with the Magners Pear Cider logo. He nodded. 'Two?' he held up two fingers and looked at Jodie. She was rocking her head back and forth to the beat and paying no attention whatsoever. I gave up and nodded back. He went to the fridges and came back with two Magnerses.

'Fourteen dollars,' he said. This was going to be an expensive nine drinks. I gave him the money.

'Hey,' I said. 'I wanted to speak to someone about my band playing here next Saturday night.'

'We don't do rooms,' he said.

I shook my head. 'No, I said *playing* here. I have a band, we want to play here.'

'Oh,' he said. 'We don't do bands.' He waved his head towards the DJ booth.

'Yeah, I know.' I said. 'But we're really good and it's my birthday. I was hoping I could book the place out.'

He shrugged. 'I don't like your chances, but I'll get Tony for you.'

He went and got Tony, who I presumed was the manager.

He appeared from an office somewhere and smiled. He was a tough-looking sort but he seemed pleasant enough. Jodie smiled at him and leant forwards on the bar a bit. The music was a bit quieter now so we could hear.

'Hey, Tony,' I said. 'I had a market stall here a few weeks ago and it was really great. It went really well. I just wanted to say I love the work you guys are doing.'

'Cheers, thanks,' he said.

'Also, I wanted to know if I could book the place out next Saturday night. It's for a party; we want to have a band.'

He thought about it.

'How many people and what time?'

I hadn't thought about that one. 'Umm, eight, I guess. And there'd be . . . eighty people.' Eighty seemed reasonable, that was fewer than twenty each. We didn't want too many people there or we wouldn't be unheard of any more.

'We're pretty busy on Saturday nights. I don't think I could do eight. You'd have to come at three.'

'In the afternoon?' I asked. That seemed a bit early.

'Yep.'

'What about seven—could you do seven?'

'I can do three,' he said.

That was way too early. No self-respecting hipster was going to come to a gig at three in the afternoon.

'You can't do a bit later than that?' I asked.

'Sorry,' Tony said.

Jodie leaned a bit closer and let her cleavage show a bit more.

'You can't do six-thirty?' She asked.

Tony wasn't fazed. 'I can do three,' he said.

Jodie batted her eyelashes a little and reached into her pocket. She pulled out a large wad of cash and put it on the bar. 'What if we made it worth your while, Tony?'

This got his attention. For a second at least.

'Is that Monopoly money?'

Jodie nodded.

He laughed.

'Look, I'll tell you what, I can let you have the place at six for an hour, but it'll cost you five hundred bucks and if you bring any fewer than eighty people I'll have to open it up to the public anyway. At seven it'll be all comers no matter what. Deal?'

This was a pretty good deal.

'Deal,' I said. 'I'm Matt, by the way.'

'What's the name of your band?' Tony asked, pulling out some paperwork from behind the bar.

'TRI△NGLR,' I said.

'Never heard of you,' he said.

I nodded.

'How do you spell it?'

It took a while to explain, but he got there in the end. 'All right, Matt, I'm going to need a deposit.'

Jodie banged the wad of Monopoly money down on the bar again. She was swaying a bit.

'I was thinking actual money,' he said. 'I need fifty per cent.' I gave him $250 and we shook hands.

We had a gig.

Now all we needed was a triangle player.

'Hey, Tony,' I said before we headed over to fight the deaf people for a spot. The music was louder again. They were playing some disco song. 'What's the most hipster drink do you reckon?'

'Trickster?' he said. Looking puzzled.

'No, *hipster*,' I repeated. 'What's the most hipster drink?'

He nodded. 'Ahh,' he said. 'Pear cider. Without a doubt.'

I knew it.

I grabbed Jodie by the arm and we headed over to find a seat.

'He was a douche,' Jodie said.

'What, Tony?' I asked.

'Yeah.'

'He seemed all right to me.'

'Did you see his tattoo?'

'No, what was it?'

'He had a southern cross on his wrist. Fascist.'

I hadn't noticed. 'Are you sure? Maybe it was something else. He seemed pretty cool to me.'

'Fascist,' she said. I shrugged.

'You know what your problem is?' Jodie asked in a huff.

I wasn't aware I had any problems. Other than caffeine poisoning. Which was a pretty minor issue now anyway. I certainly hadn't been the one vomiting in my toilet half an hour before. I pointed this out.

'You're too nice.'

This seemed like a compliment not a problem. I pointed this out also.

'You need to be more judgemental,' Jodie said. 'Hispters are judgemental.' She was slurring a bit now. It was cute.

'I'm judging you,' I said. 'Does that help?'

'No. Because I'm not a hispter.'

That didn't even make sense. She had a point though.

'I think you're pretty much the ultimate hipster now,' she said, playing with my tape necklace. 'Almost anyway: you just need to stop being such a nice guy.'

'I don't know if I can,' I said. 'I just kind of naturally am a nice guy. I don't know if I can change that.'

She shrugged. 'You're not the ultimate hispter then.'

I sighed.

'All right, well, what do I have to do then?' I asked.

'We need to go and judge some people,' she said.

'I don't know if I like that idea,' I said. 'What if they hear? I don't want them judging me back. What if I get in a fight? Fighting isn't very hipster.'

She thought about this for a while. 'Well. I know a bunch of people who aren't going to hear you,' she said.

'Who?' I asked.

She pointed at the group of deaf kids. 'C'mon, let's go and sit with them. We can pay out their shoes. It'll be fun.'

I didn't like this idea. It seemed mean, but I let her drag me along. She was kind of right. I guessed it wouldn't take very long. All I had to do was make some judgemental comments about how their jeans were too baggy and I could crown myself the ultimate hipster and get on with my life. I didn't mind the idea of getting on with my life to be honest. Being a hipster was tiring work.

We shuffled our way into the group and made it clear we wanted to sit down on one of the couches. I didn't know any sign language, but it wasn't too hard to convey what we were on about. They reluctantly shuffled over and let us in before going back to their sign language conversation.

'OK,' Jodie began. 'Let's go.' She looked for someone to judge. 'See that girl over there,' she said. 'Blue shoes. They look like she bought them at Target. Eew. Loser.' It wasn't very convincing. Jodie wasn't very good at being mean to people either.

I nodded.

'OK, your turn,' she said.

'Oh, OK, umm. Well.' I was struggling. 'That guy over there, tweed jacket, in the hat. How gay is that hat?' Jodie slapped me.

'Oh sorry. I mean, how lame is that hat?'

'That's better,' she said. 'How did that feel? Hip?'

I shrugged. It felt a bit mean to be honest—although it was a pretty gay hat. She told me to have another go.

'OK,' I said. 'Guy over there, signing something. He looks like Michael Bolton. Stupid hair.'

Jodie nodded. 'That was lame.'

'I know. I'm not very good at this.'

'I'm going to the toilet,' Jodie said. She stumbled away.

I sat there feeling a bit glum. And incredibly tired. I was supposed to be excited because I was one triangle player away from becoming the ultimate hipster and instead I was intoxicated, in a bar and paying out deaf people. I didn't want to be intoxicated and in a bar paying out deaf people. I wanted to be home in bed.

I was about to get up and wait for Jodie outside the bathroom so I could tell her I was keen to leave when a girl came and asked if the seat next to me was taken. I was going to say no, she could have it, when the pendant she was wearing caught my eye. It looked familiar. In fact it looked exactly like the one I'd sold to the cute deaf girl at the market stall. I looked at her face and realised it *was* the cute deaf girl from the market stall.

She wouldn't have recognised me because I was wearing sunglasses and a hat when we first met, but I told her the seat wasn't taken and then explained I was the one who sold her the pendant. She could lipread what I was saying just fine, but I had a bit of trouble understanding her because of the noise. We managed to have a rough conversation and she told me they were celebrating a friend's birthday. I asked what the point of having it in a bar was if you can't hear anything and she explained that not everyone was profoundly deaf, some people were just hearing impaired, but that even if you were totally deaf you could still feel the vibrations, which was kind of fun. Beethoven used to do the same thing—when he went deaf he loved to play the bass notes so he could feel them.

We had a great little chat about what music she liked and it turned out she was a big fan of grunge. We discussed how it hadn't made a proper comeback yet and I told her I was in a hipster grunge band. She thought that was cool.

And then I had an idea.

'Hey,' I said, turning to her so she could read my lips. 'Do you want to be in my band?'

'I'm deaf!' she said.

'That's the beauty of it. It's ironic! It's so hipster!'

'I can't play anything. What would I do?'

'Triangle,' I said, making a sign and then pointing to the tattoo on my wrist.

'Really?!' she asked. She was excited. 'I've never heard of a grunge band with a triangle player before.'

'Exactly!' I said. 'It's easy anyway. You can just play it in time with the kick drum!' She gave me a cute smile and put her hand on my leg.

At that moment Jodie came back.

'Hey, you gave my seat away!' she protested.

'She was cuter than you,' I yelled. 'And she offered to play triangle in my band.'

'Ah,' she nodded. 'Hey, just on that. I realised where we were going wrong before.'

'Yeah, me too,' I interrupted. 'We were hanging shit on deaf people.'

'No, not that. Well, yeah, that was a bit mean, but we weren't paying them out for having a disability, we were paying them out for having Target shoes and shit hair. That's not quite the problem though. We're supposed to be judging people for trying to be too cool. Hispters are supposed to judge other hispters, not deaf people with bad hair and Target shoes.'

I agreed. The cute deaf girl was engrossed in a sign language conversation with another friend so I decided to leave her be for a while.

'So let's give it another go, and then, since you've found your triangle player, you can officially be the ultimate hipster.'

'OK.' I said.

Jodie went first.

'OK.' She was looking around the bar for a target without a hearing impairment. 'See that guy there?' She pointed at someone with an undercut and a pink bowtie. 'Have a look at his bowtie. Could he be trying any harder? Fucking hipster.'

'That's more like it.' I said.

'Yeah, that felt good,' she said. 'Your turn.'

I looked around for a while and spied a girl across the bar wearing a fur coat. 'Oh my God,' I said. 'Check out the fucking murderer over there in the ballet flats.' I pointed. 'That is so not cool. And what happened to her fringe? Did the fox she killed fucking try to bite her face off and miss? Fucking hipster.'

'That was good.' Jodie looked impressed.

'Yeah?'

'Yeah,' she said. 'You're a natural.'

It was Jodie's turn again and she spied a girl with a dragon tattoo. That copped some shellacking. I saw a short guy wearing a beret. We called him the Paris Hipster. Then, because he was little, we shortened it to Pipster. He had a dreadlocked girlfriend who was wearing jeans so tight they looked like pantyhose so we called her Hippy Long Stockings.

'How are we doing do you think?' I asked Jodie.

'You know what, let's do one more each and then I think you are officially the world's ultimate hipster.'

This was exciting. My quest was very nearly over. I still hadn't found the ultimate hipster girlfriend, but it didn't really matter too much anyway. The cute deaf girl was wearing a vintage dress and had potential, so who knew where the night was going to lead? She still had her hand kind of near my leg.

'OK, there we go,' Jodie said. 'Take a look at the dude in the scarf over there. The chequered keffiyeh thing around his neck. I can't believe he's wearing that. Those things were so, like, 2009—even before Justin Bieber started wearing them. Fucking hispter. I bet he even listens to Justin Bieber.' It was a low blow, but fair given the circumstances. It would take some beating.

It was my turn. This was the moment I'd been waiting on for almost three months now. I rubbed my tattoo and kissed my tape necklace. I thought fixed-gear thoughts and straightened my glasses. All I needed was a target. I didn't want to pick on just anyone either: they needed to be screaming for it.

And then, out of the crowd he appeared, rolling a cigarette and pouting like a supermodel on crack.

'Jodie. Jodie, Oh my God, look over there behind you.' I pointed. She turned, almost in slow motion, to see my quarry on the other side of the bar. He was looking straight at us. 'Check out that dickhead in the fucking Fargo flap hat and waistcoat. He's drinking—'

'Don't say it!' Jodie interrupted.

'I have to!' I said.

Jodie covered her ears.

'He's drinking *apple* cider. Apple cider. Who the fuck drinks *apple* cider? That is so 2010. What a failed fucking hipster.'

Jodie applauded.

'I think your work here is done.' She gave me a hug.

I thanked her. 'You don't think I went a little over the top there with the apple cider thing?'

'It was firm, but fair.'

'I feel dirty.'

'Don't. It was for science. And really, who wears Fargo flap hats any more?'

 I nodded. Then I started to get worried.

'Umm. Hey, Jodie?' I said.

'What?'

'I think he's coming over here.'

She turned around. He was. He was pushing people out of the way to get to us and he looked pissed off. From across the bar he'd looked kind of small, but as he got closer I realised he must have been at least six foot three and he was built like a rugby player. He was looking straight at me.

I looked away and started trying to talk to the cute deaf girl again. It was no use though: he'd definitely seen me and he was coming over.

'What the fuck did you just say to me?' he said, towering over me, angry. I was still sitting down. His voice was weird. He must have been drunk. The music was loud, but I could definitely hear what he was saying.

'Hey man, nothing, I'm not sure what you mean. I was just talking to my friend here,' I said.

He lifted up the flaps over his ears to reveal a couple of large hearing aids.

'You think my hat's funny?' he said. 'Do you think it's amusing the doctors say I have to keep the wind out of my ears so I don't lose the last two per cent of my hearing?'

'No man, no, not at all. I was saying I like your hat. It's cool.'

He started talking to the cute deaf girl in sign language. Apparently they knew each other. 'Hey Cassie.' He spoke the words as well, so I could hear. 'Is this guy a friend of yours?' He flicked his head towards me.

The cute deaf girl turned to me and shrugged. She did some sign language which I couldn't understand, but she pointed to her pendant and made the shape of a triangle a little bit. She was smiling.

'Well, this guy here seems to think he's a bit cooler than everyone else. He thinks it's fun to hang shit on people for being deaf.'

She looked at me accusingly.

'That's totally not true,' I began. 'I wasn't hanging shit on anyone.'

'Mate, I can lip-read, I saw everything you said.' He signed what I'd said to him to Cassie. There was no mistaking the dickhead bit.

Cassie looked unimpressed.

I tried to explain. 'No, you've got it all wrong, I wasn't being serious. We were saying stuff to everyone, we were just joking. I don't really think you're a dickhead. I think your hat is cool.'

He explained to Cassie that we'd been sitting there judging everyone.

'Well, no, not everyone,' I said. 'Just a few people.'

Cassie spoke to him in sign language.

'Yes, well, she says she saw you pointing at a few of her other friends too,' he said.

She looked at me. 'I can't believe you would do that,' she said.

She signed to the angry guy some more and pointed at the guy with Michael Bolton hair.

'What did you say about her brother Dane over there?' the angry guy shouted. The music was pretty loud. 'He's had a pretty rough time since he hit his head in the car accident so this better be good.'

This was going from bad to worse. 'I just said he looked a bit like, well, Michael Bolton,' I said. 'But that's cool. That's ironic. Michael Bolton and, like, Lionel Ritchie's hair is, like, totally ironic 80s cool.'

The angry guy shook his head in disgust and turned to Cassie.

'What?' She was mouthing the word. I could make that out. 'What?'

'You don't want to know,' he said.

'Tell me,' she said, looking at me and then back to the angry guy.

'He said he was a fucking moron.'

Cassie threw her drink at my crotch and stormed off. Everyone in the group turned around to look at me.

'That's not what I said!' I protested. 'I said he looked like Michael Bolton. Michael Bolton!' I was slurring my words a little bit and I didn't want them to misunderstand me, so I twirled my finger near my ear to indicate Michael Bolton hair and pointed at my head a couple of times. 'Michael Bolton!' I yelled, pointing at Cassie's brother and doing the little looping sign.

A few people were gasping in horror and backing away. A security guard noticed the kerfuffle and came over to see what was happening.

'What's going on?' he asked.

Angry guy explained that I'd been harassing mentally disabled deaf people. One of the people we'd been sitting next to chimed in and said that we'd pushed her out of her seat.

The security guard looked at me, then at the damp patch on my crotch. Then at Jodie, who was swaying so much she was having trouble standing. He shook his head in disgust.

'Get out,' he said.

I tried to protest.

'Get out now, before I throw you out.'

Jodie tried to explain that we were really nice people and that we'd just been joking about a few deaf people, but she was slurring her words a bit too much and the security guard grabbed her by the arm and led her to the door.

'I don't want to see either of you two fucking hipsters in here again,' he said.

'But . . .' I protested.

He glared at me. 'Do you want me to wring your neck with that scarf?'

I said no.

And that was that. Now I had no show, no triangle player and no hope of booking anything else this late in the piece.

We sat down in the gutter up the road from the bar, despondent. Jodie was starting to fall asleep with her head on my shoulder.

'Hey,' she said. 'I almost forgot. I have this for you.'

She pulled out a little badge from her pocket. It said **Ultimate Hipster** on it.

'I made it for you. The font is Helvetica,' she said, and pinned it to my lapel. 'You've earned it. You don't need a triangle player anyway, you've already got a tattoo. That's plenty.'

I said thanks. I guessed it was fitting, but now that I'd got the badge I didn't want it. I just wanted to go back to being me, but I couldn't even do that though because I still had no idea who I was. Trying to become the ultimate hipster hadn't helped me find myself at all: it had just let me wear a costume for a while. Now I wanted to take that costume off. I wanted a hipsterectomy.

'You know where we went wrong back there?' she asked.

I could think of a few places.

'We stuck around too long,' she said. 'We should have just done a hip and run.'

I laughed. And then I sighed.

'What's wrong?' Jodie asked.

'This is shit.' I said. 'I've made it all this way, I've become the ultimate hipster and now I feel like I've just let everyone down. We haven't got a gig, I couldn't even find a triangle player, and my crowning achievement is paying out some deaf people. This journey was supposed to help me find myself, but I've done the opposite. I've gone backwards.'

She thought about this for a while. 'You haven't gone backwards,' she said. 'It's impossible to go backwards. Besides, do you honestly think anybody ever figures out who they are in this life anyway?'

I hadn't thought about that.

'You could win an Olympic gold medal, you could discover a cure for cancer, but that doesn't mean you know who you are,' she said. 'It just means you know what you've done. And when you do dumb things, when you make mistakes, it just means you've got a bit more evidence of who you're not.'

I nodded.

'And you know what you're not, Matt Granfield?'

'What?'

'You're not a fucking hipster.'

ACKNOWLEDGEMENTS

Claire Kingston at Allen and Unwin, who was responsible for the inception of this book, deserves the biggest thanks of all for having faith in my ability to make it a reality. Thank you, Claire, you are a champ and I will forever owe you a few ciders. Thank you also to the rest of the Allen and Unwin team, who have been amazing to work with. Thank you especially to my friends who made it into *HipsterMattic*: Dave (my brother) and Dave (my best friend) in particular, and to those who made it into the book but had their names changed—without you I'd be a very lonely and boring little hipster.

If you liked this, why not try more books from Allen & Unwin?

Dirty Deeds
by Mark Evans

An honest, revealing and sometimes laugh-out-loud memoir of one of Oz music's noisiest quiet achievers—Mark Evans, the original bass player from AC/DC.

A few days after his 19th birthday, rock and roll lover and bass player Mark Evans wandered into his local to check out the band—and his life would never be the same again. Two days later he was playing his first show as bass player with AC/DC; within a week he was on Countdown, rocking out next to wildman Bon Scott, who was dressed as a pigtailed, cigarette-smoking schoolgirl—and waving a mallet—and Angus who was—of course—decked out as a schoolboy. And all for the princely wage of $60 a week!

Then came nearly being burnt alive on the video shoot for 'Jailbreak', and working with legends Vanda and Young on the massive album TNT, on which Mark's take-no-prisoners basslines anchored such immortal hits as 'TNT' and 'It's a Long Way To the Top'. Within a year, the band had relocated to London and were on the road to rock 'n' roll stardom, living the life of rock gods and making the most of all that had to offer. Until the tragic death of his good friend Bon Scott changed everything.

Mosh Potatoes
by Steve Seabury

More than 100 recipes from the heavyweights of heavy metal including KISS, Judas Priest, Guns 'n' Roses and many more.

Divided into 'Opening Acts' (appetisers), 'Headliners' (mains), and 'Encores' (desserts), *Mosh Potatoes* features 147 recipes that every rock 'n' roll fan will want to devour—including some super-charged Spicy Turkey Vegetable Chipotle Chilli from Ron Thal of Guns N' Roses, Orange Tequila Shrimp from Joey Belladonna of Anthrax (complete with margarita instructions), Italian Spaghetti Sauce and Meatballs from Zakk Wylde of Black Label Society (a homemade family dish), Krakatoa Surprise from Lemmy of Motorhead (those who don't really like surprises may want to keep a fire extinguisher handy), and Star Cookies from Dave Ellefson of Megadeth.

Mosh Potatoes comes with a monster serving of backstage stories and liner notes, making this ideal for young headbangers, those who still maintain a vice-like grip on the first Black Sabbath album, and everyone who likes to eat.

Mum Had Kingswood:
Tales from the life and mind of Rosso
by Tim Ross

It's a book. A funny book. A funny book by Tim 'Rosso' Ross.
But what's in this funny book I hear you ask?

Well, it's all manner of stories from the life and mind of Tim
Ross. There are warm, fuzzy childhood stories of billycarts and
milk bars. There are teenage stories of angst, girls, bad clothes
and bad hair. There are student tales of share-house madness
and misery. And there are adults tales of living out a rock n' roll
dream, doing stand up, being on the telly and entertaining the
nation on the radio every morning.

In between all these wonderful tales, there are rants and raves,
ideas and fantastical stories. Just stuff really. Wonderful stuff
from the mind of Tim 'Rosso' Ross. This is his book. It's part
memoir, part brain dump. And he's written it just for you.

Don't Tell Mum . . .
by Paul Carter

A 'take no prisoners' approach to life has seen Paul Carter heading to some of the world's most remote, wild and dangerous places as a contractor in the oil business. Amazingly, he's survived (so far) to tell these stories from the edge of civilization, and reason.

Paul Carter has been shot at, hijacked and held hostage.

He's almost died of dysentery in Asia and toothache in Russia, watched a Texan lose his mind in the jungles of Asia, lost a lot of money backing a mouse against a scorpion in a fight to the death, and been served cocktails by an orang-utan on an ocean freighter. And that's just his day job.

Taking postings in some of the world's wildest and most remote regions, not to mention some of the roughest oil rigs on the planet, Paul has worked, gotten into trouble and been given serious talkings to in locations as far-flung as the North Sea, Middle East, Borneo and Tunisia, as exotic as Sumatera, Vietnam and Thailand, and as flat out dangerous as Columbia, Nigeria and Russia, with some of the maddest, baddest and strangest people you could ever hope not to meet.

Strap yourself in for an exhilarating, crazed, sometimes terrifying, usually bloody funny ride through one man's adventures in the oil trade.

'Great two-fisted writing from the far side of hell.' – John Birmingham, bestselling author of *He Died with a Felafel in his Hand*

'A unique look at a gritty game. Relentlessly funny and obsessively readable.' – Phillip Noyce, director of *The Quiet American* and *Clear and Present Danger*

Is That Thing Diesel?
by Paul Carter

The next eagerly awaited, high octane, seat-of-your-pants adventure from the author of the bestselling Don't Tell Mum I Work on the Rigs, She Thinks I'm a Piano Player in a Whorehouse *sees (the surely a bit bonkers) Paul Carter circumnavigating Australia on a bio-diesel motorcycle.*

At forty years old, a successful writer, husband and father, no longer toiling on offshore drilling rigs, was Paul Carter happily nestled in the cotton wool of suburban life enjoying the fruits of his labour? Was he f**k!

With his manic life left far behind and the perfect opportunity to take it easy stretched before him what else would a middle-aged, bike obsessed, man want?

Yes, that's right, he'd want to be the first guy to ride around Australia on an underpowered experimental motorcycle that runs on used cooking oil, wouldn't he? Preferably without getting hit by a semi-trailer full of bridge parts. Is he out of his mind? Quite possibly.

Embark on a rollickingly, downright dangerous and often unhinged quest that starts on an environmentally friendly motorcycle built on a shoestring budget by students, and ends with a plan to break the motorcycle land speed record for bio fuel.

Carter is back to his old balls-to-the-wall style of writing, prepare to laugh out loud.

This is not a Drill
by Paul Carter

Adrenalin junkie, oil rigger, motorbike fanatic, madman . . . Paul Carter, author of Don't Tell Mum I Work on the Rigs, She Thinks I'm a Piano Player in a Whorehouse, *is back with more (mostly) good clean stories of life on the rigs.*

He's back on the rigs and back in trouble.

Picking up right where he left off, Paul Carter pulls out more tall tales of a mad, bad and dangerous life in the international oil trade. Starting with action and mayhem galore *This Is Not A Drill* sets an unrelenting pace that just doesn't let up, as Paul almost drowns when the Russian rig he's working on begins to capsize; is reunited with his Dad—another adrenaline junkie; gets married; hangs out with his rig pig buddies in exotic locations; gets hammered on vodka in Sakhalin; and spends a couple of interesting weeks in Afghanistan with some mates who run an outfit that just happens to contract out mercenaries for hire . . .

This is the next fast, furious and very funny book from Paul Carter, the author of the bestselling *Don't Tell Mum I Work on the Rigs, She Thinks I'm a Piano Player in a Whorehouse.*

Want to find out more about the book you've just read?
Keen to find more books just like this one? Just want to keep in touch with us about forthcoming titles?

Facebook: facebook.com/pages/Allen-Unwin-Books/99174606158

Twitter: @AllenAndUnwin

Tumblr: allenandunwin.tumblr.com

Or go to www.allenandunwin.com to register for our enewsletters and keep in touch with new releases, latest new and upcoming events, competitions and giveaways.

Follow Matt Granfield in your favourite social media channel and be the first to read new work, get updates of events where you can meet Matt and get your hands on exclusive giveaways.

twitter.com/mattgranfield

facebook.com/mattgranfieldthewriter

tumblr.com/mattgranfield

Instagram: http://followgram.me/mattgranfield

As well as being a prolific Tweeter, Matt also writes one of Australia's most popular non fiction blogs. Ranging from the inane to the absurd, and occasionally the political, you can subscribe to Matt's musings for free at **www.mattgranfield.com**